Teachers as Policy Advocates

Teachers as Policy Advocates

Strategies for Collaboration and Change

May Hara and Annalee G. Good

TEACHERS COLLEGE PRESS

TEACHERS COLLEGE | COLUMBIA UNIVERSITY
NEW YORK AND LONDON

Published by Teachers College Press,® 1234 Amsterdam Avenue, New York, NY 10027

Copyright © 2023 by Teachers College, Columbia University

Front cover design by Edwin Kuo. Illustration by ajichan / iStock by Getty Images. Image of May Hara by Kayla Rice Photography. Image of Annalee G. Good by Alison Bowman.

Library of Congress Cataloging-in-Publication Data is available at loc.gov

ISBN 978-0-8077-6794-8 (paper)
ISBN 978-0-8077-6795-5 (hardcover)
ISBN 978-0-8077-8152-4 (ebook)

Printed on acid-free paper
Manufactured in the United States of America

To Mike, Margot, and Hugh, with all my love

MTH

To Colin, Gavin, and Charlotte . . . I love you, infinity.

AGG

Contents

Acknowledgments

We wish to thank the many people who contributed to the work represented in this book.

First and foremost, this work would not have been possible without the expertise, time, and partnership of the teachers with whom we collaborate in Massachusetts and Wisconsin. We do our best to do justice to the richness of their knowledge, their experience, and the depth of their professional commitment in the chapters that follow. It has been our privilege to learn with such an amazing group of educators.

We deeply appreciate the collaboration of our colleagues, including the cofacilitators in workshops and EdCamps. Special thanks go to the researchers and workshop facilitators on the WEPOP team at the University of Wisconsin–Madison, as well as to Molly Carroll, Nick Ironside, and Kate Roberts for their insights.

We are grateful for the expertise of Emily Spangler, whose wise editorial guidance moved our work forward. We also wish to thank the many others at Teachers College Press who helped bring this book to fruition, including John Bylander, Christine Crocamo, Emily Freyer, Mike Olivo, and Nancy Power, as well as peer reviewers who offered feedback on early iterations of the manuscript.

Teachers as Policy Advocates

Introduction

Teachers as Policy Advocates

In February 2018, teachers in West Virginia went on strike in protest of stagnant pay, challenging work conditions, low pension rates, and a slew of other longstanding concerns. In the months preceding the 2018 midterm elections, teachers in Oklahoma, Arizona, and Colorado followed suit. The next year, their colleagues in South Carolina and Tennessee held labor actions of their own. In 2022, another wave of teacher strikes took place, including in some of the most affluent and well-resourced districts in the country. National news outlets televised teachers on picket lines, walking out of school buildings, and protesting at state capitols. Families contended with closed schools, sometimes for multiple and consecutive days. Observers across the country watched as teachers paused instruction in the name of educational justice.

This type of activism is one that springs to mind when we talk about teacher policy advocacy: teachers forced to walk out of their classrooms by ongoing educational inequality and unsustainable working conditions. Indeed, teacher strikes have long been a powerful form of advocacy: Historically, as in recent examples, teachers' collective action has resulted in pay raises and class-size reductions. However, strikes are only one type of teacher action, and one that is prohibited by law in multiple states. Typically, teacher advocacy is constrained to two possibilities: labor actions or micro-level advocacy on behalf of individual students. But policy is too important and teachers' expertise too great to overlook other meaningful ways teachers can be policy advocates at the school, district, state, and national levels. In this book, we explore how teachers can take action for change around the educational policy issues that are most important to them, with a focus on how teachers, teacher educators, researchers, and policymakers can come together to support this engagement.

Our work in this book begins from the premise that teacher policy advocacy is vital to building the education system our youth, families, and communities deserve. We conceptualize *policy advocacy* as the diverse set of critical efforts taken by teachers to influence education policy toward equitable systems change. Our theory of action is simple: We believe collaborative engagement among teachers, teacher educators, and teacher candidates can lead to increased teacher capacity for policy advocacy, and contribute to educational policy that is more inclusive, equitable, and effective. Figure I.1 provides a visual representation of our theory of action.

We argue, therefore, that collaborative learning around policy advocacy must be at the heart of teacher professional development across the career span. *Teachers as Policy Advocates* is intended to facilitate collaboration for policy advocacy between practicing and preservice teachers, school and district administrators, teacher educators, and others who are committed to more equitable and effective educational policy.

Teacher advocacy in educational policy has far-reaching implications. Strengthening professional development for policy advocacy across preservice teacher education and the K–12 field can support closer alignment of policies with the contexts in which they are implemented, greater consistency between policy text and policy in

Figure I.1. Theory of Action for a Model of Collaborative Learning, Agency, and Advocacy

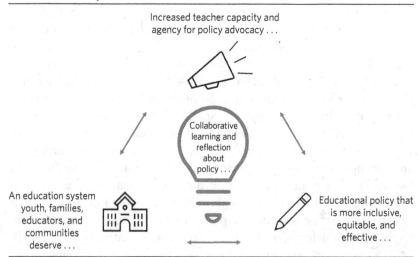

practice, and more realistic expectations for policy reforms. Teacher policy advocacy has the potential to motivate meaningful, immediate changes at the systemic level that directly impact students, schools, teachers, and the profession of teacher education. It is our hope that this book will contribute to the professional development of teachers for increased policy engagement as part of that larger mission.

The purpose, structure, and focus of this book emerged from our work over the last decade with preservice and practicing teachers in Wisconsin and Massachusetts. We have heard loud and clear the challenges that make it difficult for teachers to view policymaking as accessible, to become fully and authentically engaged in policymaking, and to embrace policy advocacy for systemic change as a component of their professional responsibilities. We were motivated by teacher conversations that took place during interviews, focus groups, and workshops to better understand which policies teachers across the career span identify as most impactful, how they make sense of these policies and their role in advocating around them, and which conditions and strategies show the most promise in supporting potential teacher policy advocacy in these areas.

OBJECTIVES

Teachers as Policy Advocates is organized around four contemporary policy topics: school safety, student assessment, public health, and digital learning, themes that emerged as important through our work with teachers in Massachusetts and Wisconsin. Policies vary in design and enactment across contexts, and individual teachers make sense of policy in a range of ways. Therefore, analyzing policies from multiple vantage points is necessary to have a nuanced understanding of how individuals in different social positions navigate and respond to policy. For that reason, the book is built around the insights of both preservice and practicing teachers across two state policy contexts, situating teachers' narratives in the literature from the fields of teacher education, teacher learning, and policy. In each policy area, we examine what teachers know about policy advocacy and how they view their relationships to advocacy.

We also seek to inform practical recommendations for supporting teacher policy advocacy and addressing organizational challenges to its success. Systemic roadblocks to teacher policy advocacy, such as limitations on infrastructure and opportunities for professional learning and leadership related to policy, are pervasive. Recognizing these roadblocks, we highlight in each chapter a specific "strategy in focus" that shows promise for increasing teacher capacity and agency for policy advocacy in the context of little support. Each of these strategies is described below.

EdCamps as Teacher-Led Professional Development. As described in Chapter 1, teachers convene day-long EdCamps as "unconferences" that center teachers as experts and prioritize connections and dialogue. They provide an authentic and collaborative professional development space that can foster greater policy advocacy among teachers by providing access to information about policies, giving teachers dedicated time and space to engage in discussion and reflection, and encouraging next steps for action. EdCamps range in the degree of time, preparation, and resources used: whether modest or ambitious in scope, virtual or face-to-face, the primary purpose is to have teachers come together in conversation as experts around policy issues that are most relevant to them. EdCamps can serve as a site for coalitions and opportunities for collaboration between teachers at local, state, and even national levels.

Collaborative Mentorship. As discussed in Chapter 2, teachers engage in a structured approach to identifying, analyzing, and potentially participating in advocacy around specific educational policies relevant in their day-to-day work. Collaborative mentorship is multidirectional, with teachers learning from one another and making sense of policy advocacy together (Ellis, Alonzo, & Nguyen, 2020; Lopez, 2013). This strategy lends itself to collaboration not only between mentoring participants but with educational researchers who can provide resources and infrastructure as they learn with and from teacher participants. While the collaborative mentorship structure described in this book was implemented through a university-based research partnership, collaborative mentorship can also be teacher-led in professional learning communities or more informal arrangements. No matter the structure, mentorship can involve teachers at multiple stages of the career span and from a range of contexts.

Coalition Building. As described in Chapter 3, teachers build connections, resources, and power with fellow teachers, families, students, unions, researchers, and community groups. Coalitions, both formal and informal, are pathways to bringing groups together for collective efforts (Greenawalt et al., 2021). In many cases, teachers already have powerful networks of information and support that can be leveraged for the specific purpose of policy advocacy. The responsibility for coalition building cannot rest solely on teachers' shoulders; policy advocacy groups, for example, can better communicate with teachers to crystallize the relevance of their policy work to practitioners' daily professional experiences. Using coalitions such as professional organizations, social media groups, parent–teacher groups, and unions as a network for policy advocacy offers unity, organization, and clout. Coalition building can be strengthened by the mapping strategy described above as teachers and others make sense of the policy landscape in their contexts.

Mapping. As outlined in Chapter 4, teachers draw "maps," or visual representations of how concepts, networks, people, organizations, and power connect to policy issues. Two different types of maps, *concept maps* and *power network maps*, are used to build teachers' understanding of policy advocacy and to facilitate actionable plans. The process centers individual experiences and beliefs, facilitates critical discussions, and provides a visual representation of ideas. Mapping is a first step to establishing the range of teachers' views and experiences regarding a specific policy issue. Teachers share their maps with a partner or a small group to identify points of convergence, resources, and areas of need. Maps and the discussions that emerge culminate in a specific action step as a springboard to future engagement, including but not limited to coalition building.

This book systematically examines contemporary educational policy issues to illustrate how preservice teachers and practicing teachers can act as policy advocates in spite of the existing obstacles to policy advocacy. We focus this examination on the following key objectives:

1. Amplify the experiences of preservice and practicing teachers with educational policy advocacy.
2. Illustrate the thought processes, actions, and viewpoints of teachers in the context of the policies they find most impactful to their work at this moment.
3. Consider the disproportionate impacts of organizational and systemic challenges on the policy advocacy of teachers with various social identities.

4. Provide evidence for the importance of collaboration in multiple forms across policy stakeholders.
5. Provide concrete examples of promising strategies for strengthening teacher policy advocacy that practitioners can apply to their own institutional, organizational, policy, and individual contexts.

We do not suggest that the "solution" to policy problems is simply for teachers to change their behavior; structural and institutional changes are necessary and are often beyond the reach of individual teachers. However, teachers can and do act as policy advocates while grappling with deeply entrenched norms, policies, and politics that serve to disempower them. We argue that an examination of strategies, structures, and conditions supportive of collaborative teacher policy advocacy can serve as an action guide for teachers across the career span and across the nation. Collaborative work between policymakers, teacher educators, and teachers has the potential to be impactful on individual and institutional levels.

CONCEPTUAL BACKGROUND

As stated above, our conceptualization of "policy advocacy" is one of efforts taken by teachers to influence education policy toward equitable systems change. This can include, but is not limited to, "public education and influencing public opinion; research for interpreting problems and suggesting preferred solutions; constituent action and public mobilizations; agenda setting and policy design; lobbying; policy implementation, monitoring, and feedback; and election-related activity" (Dubetz & de Jong, 2011, pp. 250–251).

We know that certain conditions are necessary for teachers to have robust capacity for policy advocacy. First, teachers need clarity on how policy is defined and what it looks like in practice. In our work with teachers in multiple districts and settings, a common and recurring question from teachers has been, "What exactly do you mean when you say 'policy'?" We define policy as encompassing the rules of engagement, written or unwritten, official or informal, selected by decision-makers to respond to a perceived need (see Table I.1). Policy is ubiquitous in schools, and yet it is often invisible. Framing educational practices, rules, and procedures as "just the way

Table I.1. Glossary of Key Terms

Policy	Rules of engagement, written or unwritten, official or informal, selected by decision-makers to respond to a perceived need.
Policy advocacy	A diverse set of critical efforts taken to influence education policy toward equitable systems change.
Policy agent	The power to impact a particular situation or other situations related to policy.
Teacher	Either a preservice (student) teacher who is in training, or a practicing teacher employed as staff in a school.
Teacher capacity	Knowledge, skills, dispositions, and self-efficacy, in this case with respect to policy advocacy.

things are" instead of as intentional choices made by policy decision-makers obscures the reality that policy is value-laden and legitimized through power. Teachers we have worked with often begin policy-related conversations believing that their encounters with policy are minimal, only to conclude that policy is, in fact, everywhere. Once that realization takes place, policies guiding discipline, grading, attendance, dress codes, pay scales, evaluation, and so forth, can then be seen for what they are: responses to perceived problems based on decision-makers' beliefs, values, and goals. Teachers increase their capacity for policy advocacy only when they identify the countless points of contact they have with school, district, state, and federal policy, as well as their own roles and responsibilities as policy experts, developers, and implementers.

We also know that teachers need opportunities to reflect on, discuss, and practice policy advocacy. In teacher education, there is a need for explicit training and mentorship around advocacy strategies (Catapano, 2006) and field placements that have rich policy contexts (Heineke et al., 2015). Practicing teachers, too, are more likely to see themselves as policy agents when embedded in a community of critical practitioners with whom they have a relationship (Behizadeh et al., 2017). Forms of participant-driven professional development (Good et al., 2017; Hertz, 2010) and informal avenues of professional learning via social media (Jones et al., 2017) are also opportunities for teachers to engage with, critique, and envision alternatives to policies. The kind of collaborative work we recommend in the chapters that follow requires purposeful professional development;

teacher educators, practicing teachers, and preservice teachers must learn to work together around building teacher advocacy and participatory decision-making (Coffman, 2015; Smylie, 1992; Taylor & Bogotch, 1994).

We also know that even when teachers have capacity for policy advocacy and opportunities to rehearse it, significant challenges exist. The policymaking process rarely involves teachers in any stage other than implementation. Teachers are seldom active or sustained players in the design of policy agendas (Conley, 1991; Ingersoll, 2006; Smylie, 1992; Taylor & Bogotch, 1994). Teachers are often left out of the creation of policy text, either in legislation or administrative codes at the state level, or in the development of school district rules at the local level. The reasons for this are multifactorial. Organizational obstacles to policy design include a lack of time, little opportunity to plan with peers, and obstructed access to discussing policy with administration (Good, 2019). Deeply entrenched societal norms shaping teacher behavior often restrict advocacy beyond one's own classroom walls. Intersectional identities of race, language status, and gender impact whose voices are heard and valued: Endemic racism and sexism can lead to differential access to advocacy power, capacity, and agency for teachers from historically marginalized and excluded groups. Furthermore, all individual, organizational, and systems-level barriers exist in sociopolitical context, and political discourse drives how teachers and policy topics are framed in public perception.

Given the conditions described above, we frame our analysis with a critical policy analysis lens (Ball, 2006; Marshall, 1997; Ozga, 1987; Taylor, 1997; Welton & Mansfield, 2020). Traditional approaches to policy have historically framed the policy process as value-neutral, and policy actors' behavior as largely rational and made to maximize self-interest (Chase et al., 2014). Critical policy analysis challenges the traditional view of policy change as a linear process in which knowledge and evaluation lead to better policy (Diem et al., 2014). Instead, it frames policy as value-laden and the result of historical and social contexts and relationships of power (Edmondson, 2004; Eppley, 2009; Taylor, 1997). Critical policy analysis also problematizes the traditional views of the policy process as comprising separate design and implementation phases. Rather, it theorizes a dynamic and multidimensional policy cycle emphasizing the roles of influence, meaning-making, power, and negotiation in the production and practice of policy (Ball, 1993/2006; Bowe et al., 1992).

Critical policy analysis emphasizes how policy impacts members of nondominant groups along race, ethnicity, gender, class, among other identities, and how members of those groups resist processes of domination and oppression (Anderson, 1989; Bensimon & Marshall, 2003; Gillborn, 2005; Henry, 1993; McLaren & Giarelli, 1995). By focusing on power, resources, inequality, and privilege in policy (Diem et al., 2014; Welton & Mansfield, 2020), critical policy analysis seeks to make the impact of status differentials based on identity visible, to acknowledge that policy is one way that institutional practices reinforce inequality, and to advocate for more equitable policies. Perhaps most importantly, critical policy studies center those who are closest to the work as the most important to understanding the impact of policy (Stovall, 2013).

In using a critical policy analysis lens, we seek to elucidate how educational policy is built on the values, beliefs, and interests of those with decision-making authority. The educational policy process is dynamic and unequally accessible, depending on status and proximity to power. Above all, our goal is to amplify the powerful voices of practitioners with the goal of collective action in the service of greater teacher policy advocacy. We believe that teachers are, as Welton and Mansfield remind us, "experts on their own lives who rightly should be the authority on identifying policy solutions to problems that affect their day to day" (2020, p. 5).

NATIONAL AND STATE POLICY CONTEXTS

The research and writing of this book took place at a unique time in the American education system. First, the activism of organizers and families of victims brought broader attention to the longstanding violence toward Black and African American people that continues to be a reality in the United States. The murders of Breonna Taylor, George Floyd, and Daunte Wright in 2020–2021 amplified a long history of unarmed Black men and women being killed by police (Thompson, 2021), spurred protests, and energized contentious debates nationally and abroad. In classrooms and schools across the country, enduring issues of racism and police brutality came to the fore, sometimes for the first time. The issues are far from new. Discussions of teaching, learning, and educational policy remain incomplete without explicit attention to race and racism in education and American society, and what has been termed a "racial reckoning" is but the beginning of the work that remains to be done.

Second, the COVID-19 pandemic that unfolded in the spring of 2020 had an incalculable impact on teaching, schools, students, and teachers. In mid-to-late March of that year, schools across the country closed their doors. Many students and teachers lost loved ones, and some lost their own lives. Remote learning was implemented in a variety of forms that foregrounded and exacerbated deep inequalities in the American education system and in society as a whole. As the 2020–2021 school year began, some students returned to schools with rapid testing, social distancing, and upgraded HVAC systems. Many others who had already had to navigate virtual learning with little or no material support returned to schools that were cramped, poorly ventilated, and understaffed. The variants of COVID-19 and the various spikes in infection rates that accompanied them meant that by the writing of this book in winter and spring of 2022, the pandemic was still impacting teachers and students. In addition to the immeasurable effects of the pandemic and its toll on mental health and learning, many districts faced critical staffing shortages across all roles, putting additional strain on the capacity and well-being of students, educators, and families.

Third, the political environment in the United States continues to be characterized by hostility toward public education. False claims about a fraudulent election system further deepened existing political divides and polarized attitudes about public education. Seemingly simple public health actions such as wearing a mask to prevent the spread of the virus in schools were weaponized into political tools. Further, claims of critical race theory "taking over" the K–12 curriculum continues to shape discussions of how we talk about the legacy and present-day manifestations of racism and anti-Blackness in the United States. The context and culture of the current sociopolitical period continues to destabilize public institutions like K–12 education and impact how educational policy problems are framed and policy responses constructed.

The policy contexts in individual states also have very real effects on teachers and students. In just one example, politicized debates about the role of racism in American history can translate into proposed state legislation limiting the topics and texts that American history courses include. The effect of this kind of proposed policy and enacted legislation can be enormous. Because we want to pay attention to the nuances of how teachers make sense of and navigate the interplay between national, state, and local policy, we have grounded this book within the policy contexts of two states. Focusing on two states, Massachusetts and Wisconsin, allows for a more in-depth and nuanced examination of the mechanisms at play. At the same time, it also narrows the types of policies around which we hear teacher dialogue given the demographic and political landscapes of each context. Teachers in states with higher percentages of immigrant and migrant students, for example, will necessarily have a different range of policy considerations than in Wisconsin and Massachusetts. Nonetheless, these two states present fascinating political dynamics and a rich contextual backdrop against which to explore teachers' relationships to policy advocacy.

Above all, we chose these two states because they are our homes. We live, work, vote, and raise our children here. We are deeply involved in these education systems on both professional and personal levels. These responsibilities afford us a variety of perspectives and deep connections, as well as a level of commitment to and care for what happens here.

Massachusetts

The K–12 public education system of the Commonwealth of Massachusetts has been described as one of the most successful in the nation, routinely scoring at the top of rankings of public-school systems across the country. Dropout rates are among the lowest nationwide, and Massachusetts students have performed competitively on international metrics (Khalid, 2013). At the same time, the Commonwealth's public schools continue to be highly segregated by race and socioeconomic class, even as racial and ethnic diversity in the student population grow. Standardized test scores on the Massachusetts Comprehensive Assessment System (MCAS) reflect persistent gaps across racial and English Learner lines.

In addition, there is a substantial racial and ethnic divide between the demographics of the student population and the teacher workforce. In the 2018–2019 academic year, there were 962,000 students enrolled in schools across Massachusetts (Massachusetts Department of Education, 2022). Of these, 59% identified as White, 9.1% identified as Black, 20.7% identified as Hispanic, and 6.9% identified as Asian. The teacher population in the state, as in much of the nation, remains largely White and female. While approximately 40% of the students in Massachusetts public schools identify as Black, Indigenous, and/or people of color (BIPOC), this is true of only 10% of Massachusetts educators. In response, the state has adopted multiple initiatives intended to increase the diversity of the teacher pool and pipeline.

School districts in the state are established along localities and are governed by locally elected school boards and superintendents. K–12 public education in the state is divided into over 400 districts comprising more than 1,800 schools. Funding for these schools, as for many across the country, depends on federal, state, and local sources. Massachusetts calculates each district's "foundation budget" as the minimum amount required to run an "acceptable" school system. The state adjusts this budget for cost of living and the ability of each district to meet the foundation threshold. Because property tax contributions range widely, there is significant variation in financial resources across urban centers and rural areas. On average, school districts spend approximately $16,000 per pupil each year, though this number varies considerably from district to district and rises to $25,000 in some localities.

Wisconsin

The public education system in Wisconsin serves over 850,000 students across 421 districts, with 69% identifying as White, 13% as Hispanic, 9% as Black or African American, 4% as Asian, 1% as American Indian, and 4% as two or more races or ethnicities (Wisconsin Department of Public Instruction, 2020). There are over 60,000 teachers in the state, with about 95% of them identifying as White (Wisconsin Educator Effectiveness Research Partnership, 2019). The largest school district in the state is Milwaukee Public Schools (serving about 78,000 students), followed by Madison Metropolitan School District (serving about 27,000 students). Wisconsin has consistently had some of the largest disparities in educational opportunities and outcomes among students from different racial and ethnic backgrounds. For example, the gap in proficiency levels on the National Assessment of Educational Progress (NAEP) between Black and White students in Wisconsin was the worst in the nation in 2019, with no meaningful narrowing of this gap over the last 10 years (Kremer, 2019).

The political environment in Wisconsin is sharply divided, playing out within debates and policy actions within the state legislature, as well as tensions between the legislature and executive branch. Educational governance in Wisconsin is divided between the state legislature, the Wisconsin Department of Public Instruction (DPI), and local school districts and boards. The state is also divided into a regional technical assistance network of 12 Cooperative Educational Service Agencies. There is a long history of "local control" discourse and norms in Wisconsin, with decision-making being decentralized to the local level, although that has diminished over the past 30 years with the state legislature passing policies such as revenue caps or more recent attempts to control local curriculum. Wisconsin often is described as one of the incubators of the school choice movement, especially with the creation of the voucher program in Milwaukee in 1989. The state made dramatic cuts to public education funding in 2011, with districts still receiving less state aid in 2021 than prior to 2011. Today, the average per pupil spending in Wisconsin is approximately $14,000.

METHODS

The data in this book was gathered over a time frame beginning in 2017 and ending in early 2022 and emerges from research along two primary threads. In Wisconsin, we learned from a series of one-time, structured and teacher-directed small-group discussions relating to specific policy topics and advocacy skills, as well as a preservice workshop model on the foundations of policy advocacy. In Massachusetts, we explored what happens with preservice and practicing teachers engaged in a sustained mentorship learning experience focused on policy and policy advocacy. This mentorship model included workshops on the foundations of policy advocacy, partner discussions, and reflective memos. In addition, the data from Chapter 1 emerged from a larger, longitudinal study of collaborative discussions around policy among a group of Massachusetts preservice teachers. In our analysis across all three sets of data, we draw upon teachers' written and spoken reflections, survey responses, individual interviews, self-reflection surveys, samples of collaborative writing, and other artifacts.

In total, we learned from the experiences of over 100 teachers across two state contexts. These teachers include preservice, novice and veteran educators, urban, rural, and suburban districts, highly resourced and under-resourced schools, and heterogeneous and homogeneous student populations. We purposefully include in the book the experiences and viewpoints of both preservice and practicing teachers. Student teaching has long been understood to be a critical period for the development of pedagogical practices and new ways of thinking about teaching and learning. However, the student teaching practicum merits more attention as a time when student teachers develop beliefs, attitudes, and skills relating to educational policy. Positioned between the roles of apprentice and full-fledged teacher, as well as between the geographic spaces of the K–12 and university classrooms, preservice teachers play different roles in the various institutional contexts they inhabit. In spite of their distinct vantage point, teachers are unlikely to report high levels of self-efficacy relating to policy and are especially unlikely to be involved in advocacy (Good et al., 2020). We interlace the views and experiences of preservice and practicing teachers to offer a more complete and nuanced understanding of teachers and policy advocacy over the timeline of a career. Throughout the book, we use preservice and practicing teachers' own words to relay their thoughts, concerns, and wonderings whenever possible. Since the nature of our work in Wisconsin was in one-time or two-time interactions with larger groups of teachers in workshop settings, we use their voices to consider broad themes from this larger sample of teachers across various workshop contexts. Conversely, our work in Massachusetts with smaller groups of teachers over the course of multiple months allowed for sustained interaction. Therefore, when drawing on the voices of teachers in Massachusetts, we at times identify specific individuals, using pseudonyms for the teachers and their school districts.

Our sample reflects broader national demographics in teaching, which means the majority of teachers whose experiences are reflected in these chapters identify as White and female. Though our analysis reveals consistent patterns of teacher experience, behavior, concerns, and needs, as well as differences across location, level of training, and individual experience, we are acutely aware that the perspectives in this book cannot be a complete portrayal of teacher policy advocacy without more robust racial, ethnic, and other forms of diversity. We are equally aware of how our own identities as an Asian American, cisgender woman researcher and a White, cisgender woman researcher necessarily impacted our research and writing processes. As former K–12 teachers and current researchers and teacher educators focused on centering social justice and equity in all aspects of our work, we continue to strive for greater representation of traditionally underrepresented and historically marginalized educators, not only in research, but also in classrooms across the country.

A note on reciprocity: We sought to develop authentic, respectful, mutually supportive relationships with the teacher-participants in our studies. The teachers who gave of their time, experiences, and reflections did so for a variety of reasons, not least of which was a deep commitment to professional development and the field of education. Nevertheless, given that none of the analysis in this book could exist without their contributions, it was critically important to us as researchers that, however possible, we compensate them for their efforts. As a result, the preservice and practicing teachers in the Massachusetts collaborative mentorship study received a stipend for their participation in the collaborative mentorship experience. We offered participants the opportunity to review and offer feedback on data analysis, as well as on early stages of written work that resulted from our collaboration. The practicing teachers in Wisconsin involved in cofacilitating policy workshops with preservice teachers were provided a stipend, while the preservice teachers in Wisconsin were not financially compensated because the workshops were part of their already existing coursework for which they received credit. Similarly, those in the Massachusetts preservice teacher cohort highlighted in Chapter 1 were not financially compensated. Whenever possible and appropriate, we supported participants in the preservice-only group by providing professional advice and resources. In addition, we collaborated with practicing teachers and teacher educators outside of the original studies to solicit their perspectives on our emerging themes and the showcased strategies, critical work for which they were also compensated. And as we have done in the past, we will continue to bring back our written work to share with districts, teacher education programs, and groups of teachers interested in thinking and talking about policy.

HOW TO USE THIS BOOK

This is primarily a book *about* practitioners *for* practitioners. We believe that *Teachers as Policy Advocates* lends itself to multiple uses in the teacher education and the K–12 contexts, including but not limited to undergraduate teacher education classes, graduate courses in education and policy, practicing teachers' professional learning communities, and district and school administrators' reading lists. In the spirit and practice of collaborative professional development, our hope is that readers will use the book across stakeholder groups, such as in supervising teacher–preservice teacher dyads or university researcher–classroom teacher research teams. Above all, our goal is for the book to be used to engage deeply and critically with policy advocacy across teacher education and K–12 settings with the purpose of application to practice. The book is designed to be read as a whole or in individual chapters as stand-alone case studies. The chapters may be read in or out of sequence, although Chapters 3 and 4 have overlapping themes. Each chapter showcases a "strategy in focus" presented in the context of a specific policy issue identified by teachers as especially impactful in their professional lives. We close each chapter with a set of discussion questions intended to generate thoughtful, authentic dialogue and reflection around problems of policy applicable to all readers.

Chapter 1 addresses school safety. Specifically, it focuses on proposed student discipline records policy in Wisconsin and school shooting policy in Massachusetts, contextualized in the national trends around school safety and discipline policy nationwide. We pay close attention in this chapter to racial discourse in school safety policy, drawing on reflections and discussion among teachers about how the policy frames certain youth as threats and how it has a disproportionate impact on BIPOC students, particularly Black and Brown students. We discuss themes of efficacy, race, mental health, and the teacher–student relationship as central to how teachers think about safety and discipline policies. We close the chapter with attention to a form of teacher-led "unconferences" called EdCamps as a strategy for increasing teacher capacity for policy learning and advocacy.

Chapter 2 focuses on assessment policy in Massachusetts and Wisconsin at the state, district, and school levels. In this chapter, we highlight the ways that assessment policies are entwined with discourses around rigor, equity, educational quality, and standards. We bring a critical lens to how these discourses impact perceptions of public education and of those who work in our public K–12 schools. We describe how teachers experience the negative effects of high-stakes standardized assessment policy in their teaching and relational work. We end the chapter with a focus on collaborative mentorship as a strategy for increasing teacher capacity for policy advocacy.

Chapter 3 centers on policies relating to the COVID-19 public health pandemic. We describe how preservice and mentor teachers made sense of and responded to COVID-19–related policy as it unfolded during 2020–2022. We highlight the relationship between pandemic-driven policy and the gendered nature of teaching as a "caring" profession and its implications for women teachers. We close the chapter by showcasing coalition building as a strategy in focus for increasing teacher capacity for policy advocacy.

Chapter 4 describes the case of school, district, and state policies relating to digital tools, including hardware, software, and Internet access. We examine the distribution of resources and relationships of inequality and privilege as key factors in digital tool policy, with a particular focus on the amplification of their impact in the context of the COVID-19 pandemic. We close the chapter with a focus on mapping of knowledge, networks, and other resources as a strategy in focus for increasing teacher capacity for policy advocacy.

In Chapter 5, our concluding chapter, we offer a model for how organizations, including schools, districts, teacher education programs, and state education agencies, can better organize to build the capacity of teachers to advocate around educational policy. We emphasize the importance of teacher policy engagement at all points of the policy cycle but focus on policy advocacy for systemic change in how we do the work of schooling. Our proposed model for collaborative training for teacher policy advocacy does not only acknowledge the persistent systemic and institutional challenges that make teacher policy advocacy challenging but is expressly designed to be implemented in the midst of those challenges. We offer actionable recommendations and resources emerging from the lived experiences of teachers to offer a model for advocacy toward policy that is accessible, responsive, and equitable for all students, families, and communities.

As we have already discussed, the COVID-19 pandemic and its impacts play a leading role in many of the chapters in this book. There could be no way to faithfully represent teachers' experiences in the time-frame of this study without a discussion of how the crisis continues to shape every policy decision relating to schools. COVID-19 uncovered policy silences, inconsistencies, and inequalities that already existed and, in many cases, worsened them. Therefore, while only Chapter 3 is explicitly focused on policies directly intended to respond to the coronavirus in schools, multiple chapters speak to COVID-19's influence on educational policy in some way.

Policy affects the structures, processes, and outcomes of all societal institutions, as well as the prospects of democracy in general. In the current sociopolitical climate in the United States, characterized by distrust of public schools, growing centralization of education systems, and the increasingly complex landscape of students' lives, teacher input is more important than ever. Throughout this book, you will hear the voices of teachers as they show their strategic understanding of policy problems, the barriers to implementation, and the clear impact of policy on students. We center the voices of teachers not only because we affirm their expertise, but also because we believe collaborative teacher policy advocacy can contribute to "radical democracy," where teachers, along with students, families, and communities, "work together to make things happen, rather than to have things done to them" (Gale and Densmore, 2003, p. 2).

CHAPTER 1

School Safety and Discipline Policies

> Just in general, I try not to escalate anything. And if I notice a student getting frustrated, or maybe I've been prodding too much, I'll step away rather than continue to harp on them about something. My goal is to de-escalate everything. If I notice a student getting frustrated, even if I would like them not to be frustrated and would like them to be doing something else, you have to think about "What will happen if I keep doing this?"
>
> —High school English student teacher, Massachusetts

Safety is an issue of critical importance for teachers and students in classrooms across the country. This chapter explores school safety policy from two different policy angles and with two groups of teachers at differing points in their career trajectories. Our goal is to illustrate the complexity of the concept of school safety and to show how preservice and practicing teachers experience policies relating to safety and discipline in schools. The narratives in this chapter illustrate the nuanced analysis that both preservice and practicing teachers bring to their sensemaking around school safety policies. The teachers in our groups viewed school safety to be a policy problem of paramount importance in which pedagogy, racism, and societal inequality intersect.

We examine school safety through two related areas of educational policy that are powerfully impactful in and out of schools. The first policy context is policy, both proposed and enacted, relating to school shootings in Massachusetts. Though "school safety" has historically referred to students' social-emotional well-being and efforts to address behavioral challenges in the classroom, in recent decades the concept has expanded to include the threat of school shootings. The data in this chapter draws from a larger qualitative study in which five preservice teachers placed in schools across Central and Eastern Massachusetts engaged in interviews, group discussions, and reflective memos focusing on their experiences with policies relating to school lockdowns and school shootings in their student teaching placements (Hara, 2020).

The second policy context is the "Teacher Protection Act" proposed in the Wisconsin 2017–2018 legislative session, which received considerable public attention and debate before ultimately failing to become legislation. The act included provisions relating to reporting requirements for schools and local police, expanded powers for teachers and schools to access discipline records outside of school, and teachers' options for safety-related employment issues.

Although we researched two different aspects of school safety policy in two states and with teachers in different phases of their careers, common threads help us to see the importance of these policies' underlying theories of action: the "problem" they are designed to address, the mechanisms for implementation, and the focus populations. In both the Wisconsin and Massachusetts contexts, we examine how policy text and discourses frame school safety and discipline and what solutions policy designers and implementers propose and enact.

The data shows that teachers are eager for change in this policy area. As school violence persists, as the school-to-prison pipeline worsens, and as public attention to racial injustice grows, teacher advocacy in these policy areas continues to be of critical importance. We propose in this chapter teacher-driven professional development in the form of EdCamps as a strategy for supporting teacher policy advocacy. EdCamps are "unconferences," where sessions are proposed and led by teachers, and participants are encouraged to "vote with their feet" by entering and exiting sessions most relevant and useful to their individual needs (Hertz, 2010; see https://digitalpromise.org /edcamp/). EdCamps are a powerful model for teacher reflection and professional learning. Because they are teacher-directed, they center teachers as experts and prioritize connections and dialogue in person and via digital platforms. We believe that collaborative professional development like EdCamps can build the capacity of teachers to be active participants in policy advocacy around issues that are most pressing in the current educational landscape, such as those directly affecting physical safety and emotional well-being.

In the sections that follow, we describe the policy contexts, processes of teacher sensemaking, and barriers to teacher policy engagement in the areas of school-shooting and school-discipline policies. We argue that the EdCamp model has potential to provide a powerful response to the policy needs described by novice and practicing teachers in this chapter by creating sustainable connections between teachers, by building knowledge around policy, and by building pathways to action.

TEACHERS FRAME THE POLICY CONTEXTS

In workshops, focus groups, and dyads, the teachers we worked with in Massachusetts and Wisconsin engaged in critical inquiry around the underlying foundations of proposed and enacted school safety and discipline policies. In their respective sites, teachers first analyzed the assumptions, values, and beliefs informing the policy "problem" framed in both school safety policies in Massachusetts and the proposed Teacher Protection Act in Wisconsin. They then critically examined the underlying theories of action that paved the way for specific policy solutions. In the sections that follow, we outline teachers' inquiry, reflections, beliefs, and wonderings.

School Safety Policy

Public concern about school shootings has led to a variety of proposed and enacted policy solutions (Borum et al., 2009; Jekielek et al., 2007). These policy solutions range widely in design and in implementation across districts and schools nationwide, and they have been bolstered by federal policies such as the STOP School Violence Act passed in 2018 (Ujifusa, 2018) as well as other, more recent proposed federal policy initiatives.

Those who have visited a public school in the United States in the recent past are no doubt familiar with the most visible manifestations of attempts to prevent school shootings. As stated above, these efforts vary according to state and district contexts. In the Massachusetts case, variations also existed based on grade level. The Massachusetts preservice teachers in this group who were placed in high schools described measures including restricting outside access to school buildings through buzzer systems, sign-in sheets and identification checks for visitors, checking bags for weapons within the school building, and increased surveillance in the form of school resource officers (Addington, 2009). Though teachers working in elementary schools in Massachusetts did not always report having the same scope of safety interventions as their counterparts in high schools, their schools did have locked-door and identification-check policies in place.

Within the context of the United States, Massachusetts gun policies are among the more stringent, with gun owners subject to background checks and licensing requirements. Assault weapons are banned, and additional restrictions include a "red flag" law allowing judges to block firearms possession for individuals considered to be a risk to themselves or others (Massachusetts Gen. Laws Ch 140, § 121–131Q, 2014). Preservice teachers in the Massachusetts group, however, remained deeply concerned about the possibility of a school shooting in their buildings. One teacher explained, "For me, at least, it's a constant thing. Not all day, every day, but at least once during that day you think 'Wow, this could be a reality.'" Another agreed, saying, "Yes. I think about it all the time."

One contributing factor to their concern was that none of the preservice teachers had been informed about an official policy establishing a protocol in the event of a school shooting (Hara, 2020). One elementary teacher explained:

> There's no building protocol as far as I know. [A few teachers] went to [some training]. I forget what it was called, but they did go to something. ALICE? Yes, that's what it was. They went to that and that's what they were talking about. And they said they should have that for the whole school. I agree. There should be something for the whole school.

The preservice teacher quoted above expressed surprise that only some teachers had attended the training, which is designed to prepare educators and others to respond in the event of an active shooter. She also felt uneasy that she had only known about the training because of a casual conversation during lunch.

Another high school teacher described his experience as follows:

> I met with my teacher before I started student teaching, and we went through the checklist and when we got to that part about drills, [or]lockdowns, [or] shooter safety drills, she said "We don't do those here." In terms of an official policy being explained to me, I've not heard one.

Preservice teachers were conflicted about the absence of a codified school shooting policy. On one hand, they were tempted to interpret this silence as evidence of district and school administrators' lack of concern about teachers' fears. On the other, the majority of preservice teachers in this group were wary of policy responses such as the active shooter training described by the preservice teacher quoted in an earlier section. They were aware through social media of such training being implemented more widely in other districts across the country. One student teacher said, "I would be completely traumatized by that. Either as the person roleplaying the shooter or as a victim. I refuse to believe that's the best way we have."

Preservice teachers were equally troubled by the ongoing national debate around policies allowing school personnel to carry guns in schools (Hara, 2020). The debate has gained significant traction in the years since this data was gathered. The teachers in this group took a variety of stances on gun control as a whole, ranging from strong support of gun control to describing their stances as "uncertain." However, all held the view that proposals to arm teachers in schools were unacceptable. One preservice teacher cited her religious belief as one of several factors in why she would never carry a weapon in the classroom. She explained, "I do not ever want to hold a life in my hands. . . . I don't feel like I would ever want to be in close proximity to a gun or hold it. I do not want to be armed. I would not feel safe if I had a gun."

Preservice teachers interpreted the proposal to arm teachers in two ways: first, as a fundamental distortion of teacher professional responsibility, and second, as a manifestation of a societal lack of respect for the work of teachers (Hara, 2020). One teacher said, "Arming teachers? I don't know what people are thinking. I don't feel like it's my job to use a gun to kill someone who's coming into my school." Another preservice teacher added, "It kind of makes me feel like they don't take our job as educators serious enough, because if they took that part serious they would already think, "OK, they already have so much on their plates, they already are responsible for so much, this isn't something we should add to them."

Since the data in this chapter was collected, the national conversation relating to arming teachers has evolved. In some parts of the country, legislation has loosened gun access in schools, including a bill signed by the governor of Ohio allowing teachers to carry guns after only 24 hours of training instead of the previous 700-hour requirement (Everytown for Gun Safety, 2022). In the months following the murder of 19 students and two teachers at Robb Elementary School in Uvalde, Texas, however, new gun control legislation has been passed, both nationally and in individual states. As of this writing, 33 states had policies in place to bar educators from carrying weapons within school buildings.

In the Massachusetts group, preservice teachers' exposure to school-shooting policy came in three forms: first, through enacted policies including placement of school resource officers, limiting of outside access to school buildings, and checking personal belongings; second, the absence of official policy relating to building-wide policy outlining procedures in the event of a school shooting; and third, nationally proposed and adopted policies of active shooter drills or arming teachers. In their analysis, preservice teachers identified the threat of school shootings as a significant safety concern. They raised questions about the absence of official policy relating to how to keep themselves and their students safe in the event of an active shooter. At the same time, they challenged the underlying assumptions behind existing policies for school lockdown simulations or proposed policies to arm teachers as efficacious solutions to school shootings (Hara, 2020).

The Teacher Protection Act

The Teacher Protection Act, proposed in the Wisconsin 2017–2018 legislative session, was presented as a way to increase teachers' access to information and options for protecting their physical safety in schools. The proposed legislation, which was never passed, included the following provisions:

1. Require the state Department of Public Instruction to post a summary of teachers' rights and protections under state and federal law on its website and require districts to provide the information to teachers annually.
2. Require districts to retain behavioral records of students while enrolled, and for a period after their withdrawal.
3. Expand the right to review current student behavioral records, already available to public school teachers, to those in charter and private schools.
4. Require law enforcement agencies in most cases to notify a public or private school when a student commits or is arrested for a felony or violent misdemeanor. Require schools to provide that information to teachers who work directly with that student.

5. Require schools to report physical assaults or violent crimes against teachers on school property or at school events to police within 24 hours of being notified if requested by the adult victim or adult witness of the assault.
6. Allow teachers to remove a student for 2 days after an incident.
7. Allow teachers to terminate their contracts without penalty if they are victims of violent offenses or physical assaults.
8. Require schools to provide assistance for leave and loss benefits for public school employees who are victims of physical assault or a violent crime.
9. Allow a teacher to request a suspension hearing for a student if the school administration chooses not to pursue suspension.

The Teacher Protection Act was one example of state and local policies across the country presented as an answer to school discipline problems. Throughout the 2017–2018 legislative session the bill was hotly debated in the public, with the Department of Public Instruction, disability rights groups, and the largest union in the state voicing concern or opposition. Critics of proposals similar to the TPA point to their direct connection to the school-to-prison pipeline, arguing that policies such as those promoting "zero tolerance," penalties for truancy, or increased police presence in schools tend to offer solutions for school discipline problems that involve the criminalization of students (American Civil Liberties Union, n.d.; Scott & Grant, 2016).

Comments from the head of the Milwaukee Teachers Education Association illustrate much of the central pushback to the bill from these groups: "This bill would without a doubt funnel more vulnerable children into the criminal justice system—especially students with special education needs who are already statistically at a much higher risk of incarceration" (Johnson, 2017). On the other hand, the bill's sponsor argued, "What truly grows the 'school-to-prison pipeline' is the current trend towards minimizing serious negative behavior and coddling children with no serious consequences," and was joined in support of the bill by conservative groups in the state such as the McIver Institute (Lisowski, 2018).

In the midst of the legislative session and public debate around the Teacher Protection Act in 2017, practicing teachers in Wisconsin engaged in two separate discussions of the Teacher Protection Act in the context of a teacher-directed EdCamp unconference. In the two

Wisconsin EdCamps, a small group of former teachers and current educational policy researchers from the University of Wisconsin–Madison walked up to the microphone and proposed a session with the following description:

> A bill called the "Teacher Protection Act" or AB 693 is moving
> through the Wisconsin State Assembly. What problems (if any)
> does it address and what are its possible effects on students and
> teachers? How can teachers shape policies around discipline
> at the building, local and state level? And since teachers
> have expertise, experience and opinions on policies like AB 693,
> we will talk a bit about how to write an op-ed. Come join us!

Once assigned a room and time slot for a session titled, "Teacher Voice on Student Discipline Policy and the Teacher Protection Act (AB 693)," participants walked down the long hallways of the high school where the conference was being held, set up a circle of chairs and desks, and quickly logged onto Twitter and Google to add to the discussion and collaborative notes during the session. Many of the teachers in the session had heard of the Teacher Protection Act through the media but had not yet closely explored the policy's specific provisions. As more teachers became familiar with the details of the policy, they drew on their own experiences to analyze elements and implications of the policy. Applying ideas from the policy discussion to examples from their own classrooms, they engaged in collective sensemaking (Coburn, 2001), reflecting together on what it might look like in practice if enacted. At the end of each session, groups shared resources for engaging in policy advocacy, such as finding and contacting one's state legislator and the process for writing an opinion or editorial piece about a specific policy.

Through this discussion, teachers raised questions about the policy's underlying theory of action, and in particular the problem that the policy was designed to address. In analyzing the Teacher Protection Act, they wondered: Who is to be feared, and for what? A teacher wondered how some of the language in the bill would be parsed, asking, "What is an 'incident'?" Others noted that the very title of the bill framed youth as dangerous, with one teacher characterizing the policy as "another way to criminalize being a kid." Though the policy title spoke to "teacher protection," some teachers worried that the policy's theory of action could lead to similar data being collected and reported on about teachers' lives outside of school.

Teachers in Wisconsin viewed discipline and safety as high priorities, but they understood that only good policy can effectively address complex issues. Because of this, they were skeptical about the theory of action behind the Teacher Protection Act. They questioned the underlying assumptions informing the proposed policy solution to the problem of feeling and being unsafe in schools. In particular, they challenged the foundational idea that, as one teacher described it, "a lack of student privacy protects teachers."

In the spring of 2018, a much-narrowed scope of the bill passed only the state assembly. The revised bill would have allowed teachers physically injured by a student to terminate their teaching contract without financial penalty. It was never voted on by the state Senate and therefore no elements of the bill were ever enacted.

TEACHER SENSEMAKING AROUND SAFETY AND DISCIPLINE POLICIES

Four overarching themes emerged as critical to teachers' understanding, analysis, and assessment of safety and discipline policies in their respective sites: the paucity of evidence for the policies as designed and proposed; the problematic connection between the policies and racism; the negative impact of policies on relationships between teachers and students; and the ramifications of policies for students with mental health challenges.

Efficacy and Evidence Base for Policy

In both Massachusetts and Wisconsin, teachers questioned the efficacy and evidence base behind proposed and enacted policies. The use of security personnel, backpack checks, and locked doors are highly visible policy approaches to prevention in many schools (Maguire et al., 2015). But their enactment, as with all policies, can differ widely. At one of the Massachusetts preservice teachers' schools, for example, the intended policy was for doors to be locked immediately after the final bus safely delivered its young charges to school. On one weekday morning, however, long after the parking lot was clear, a group of visitors arriving separately entered the building one after the other. Each visitor held the door open for the person behind them, thereby circumventing the raspy intercom and laminated sign requesting that visitors ring the bell and identify themselves to be buzzed in for entry.

In addition to variations in implementation, preservice teachers questioned the evidence base for the security measures instituted in their school sites (Hara, 2020). One high school teacher said, "We have one school resource officer. It doesn't make me feel safer that 'Officer Joe' is there to handle the situation. And I don't know what 'handling the situation' would look like." Preservice teachers wondered if the adoption of some unproven policies and the complacency they might engender could preclude other, evidence-based policies from being discussed, proposed, and enacted.

Teachers in Wisconsin engaged in discussion about the Teacher Protection Act had similar questions about the efficacy of the bill to address the problem of physical safety in schools. First, they wanted more information about the evidence supporting the adoption of the policy itself. One teacher wondered, "What evidence is there that says we should have this information?" with a specific query about whether the policy in its proposed iteration was "data-driven."

Second, Wisconsin teachers questioned the fit between the "problem" and the policy as an effective solution. In a group of teachers discussing not feeling completely safe in their own classrooms, one high school teacher wondered whether it would actually be valuable to know if a student "is violent or has tendencies" through access to records from outside the school setting. The group probed deeper into the intended outcome of having the type of information proposed by the Teacher Protection Act. For example, one teacher asked, "What is the teacher supposed to do differently if they have this information?," prompting others in the group to consider the actual relationship between this information and their own protection. They also wondered about unintended consequences of access to this information, with another teacher wondering aloud, "How does having [this information] make me a different teacher?"

As the data above demonstrates, teachers in both Wisconsin and Massachusetts had concerns about the evidence base for the safety and discipline policies proposed and adopted in their states and districts. They had questions about what data drives policy design, how teachers might have better access to data as a whole, and whether data supports the fit of a policy problem and its proposed solution.

Safety and Discipline Policies and Race

Practicing and preservice teachers were not only skeptical about the efficacy of school safety policies relating to shootings and discipline, but also expressed concerns about the impact of policy responses on pre-existing inequities relating to power, authority, and control in schools. These concerns are supported by research demonstrating, for example, that the presence of school resource officers and metal detectors not only increases students' view of school as punitive (Noguera, 1995) but also contributes to higher rates of student victimization (Schreck & Miller, 2003) and instances of violations of student privacy (Addington, 2009).

The data presented in this chapter were gathered primarily in the 2018–2019 academic year, at the beginning of what would develop into an intense wave in support of racial equity and justice in the United States. Though violence and racism against students of color, particularly Black and Brown students, has been a constant in American education since its beginnings, the grassroots movement for more honest conversations about race, racism, and schools was galvanized by the murders of George Floyd and many others.

The Massachusetts preservice teachers were especially troubled by the impact of school safety policy on students already systematically and historically marginalized in schools (Hara, 2020). They believed that the potential harmful effects of school safety policy on BIPOC students would outweigh potential benefits, particularly in the absence of clear data demonstrating the efficacy of the policy approaches to improving the level of safety in their schools. Tom is a White male teacher who entered the teaching profession after a prior career in a different sector. His preservice placement was in a small, urban high school serving a predominantly African American and Latinx student body. He shared his emerging concerns about school safety policies informed by ongoing explorations of authority, justice, and equity in education in apprenticeship to his supervising teacher, an African American woman who identified strongly as a social justice–driven educator. Tom raised the question of how security measures might impact his students, especially given national data indicating deep-seated racial inequity in the criminal justice system as a whole. He explained: "When you have metal detectors? And you have armed guards at school? It just sounds like a prison to me. Anything you can do to make school less like a prison—you can point to the rigid schedule, the authority figure, only being able to go to the bathroom at a certain time. . . ."

Some Wisconsin teachers raised similar concerns about the intersection between school discipline policies and racism. They felt that the provisions in the Teacher Protection Act reflected a view of schools as dangerous. Teachers challenged this view and noted the ways in which notions of "danger" and "safety" in schools are often entangled with race, leading to an interpretation of schools as dangerous if Black and Brown students are involved. One teacher stated, "A comment like 'I don't feel safe' is a proxy for a racial comment." Teachers expressed concern that some of the provisions in the Teacher Protection Act could actively compound stigma and create negative narratives around specific students, particularly those from historically marginalized groups. Others agreed that being able to see records demonstrating past disciplinary infractions or violence would inevitably lead to bias against students already more likely to be racially profiled in schools.

Teachers were also concerned that the power to give suspensions would increase under this bill, especially given patterns in disproportionate discipline actions against students of color and students with disabilities in their school districts. A teacher in the EdCamp session questioned, "If this is only for some crimes, how does that disproportionately marginalize who we are criminalizing?" Another teacher reflected on the issue of disproportionality specifically in the context of Milwaukee Public Schools (MPS), which is the largest urban school district in the state, serves a large percentage of students of color, and has a long history of racialized suspensions. Indeed, the federal Office of Civil Rights investigated, issued a report, and signed a settlement with MPS mandating their plans for addressing disproportionality in disciplinary actions. Suspensions have subsequently decreased.

Teachers in both Wisconsin and Massachusetts saw clearly the connection between safety and discipline measures and the long, ongoing history of racism and discrimination in schools. These teachers were already well aware of the deep roots of racism entwined in the concepts of safety, danger, and discipline. They had questions about the motivations behind and the implications of school policy relating to safety. Further, they called out the notion of "neutral" policies that actually disproportionately impact students of color, identifying school safety and discipline policies alongside others that discriminate against particular racial, ethnic, and gender identities (Aghasaleh, 2018; Knipp & Stevenson, 2021). The majority-White teachers in our groups had serious concerns about their complicity in larger systems of racist practices by implementing such policies.

Since data collection for this chapter concluded, public debate around the role of race in our schools has continued to be contentious and polarized. Most recently, some school districts received calls for the removal of teaching perceived as Critical Race Theory (CRT) from K–12 curriculum and instruction. The discourse and proposed state legislation in states such as Wisconsin have shown not only a lack of basic understanding of CRT, but a direct refusal to recognize racism as central to American history and society. It is in this climate that teachers raise questions about policies that are presented as race neutral. Any discussion of school discipline, school safety, and other policies that have a disproportionate impact on students of color must be situated in the larger context of ongoing battles relating to racial equity in schools.

Impact on Relationships Between Teachers and Students

A third important theme for practicing and preservice teachers in Wisconsin and Massachusetts related to how school safety policies not only failed to recognize the importance of relationships in class-rooms, but in many cases actively created barriers to positive, sustain-ing connections between teachers and students.

Preservice teachers in the Massachusetts group viewed the tasks of fostering trust and connection with students, as well as encouraging personal growth, as among the most important of their professional responsibilities (Hara, 2020). As described earlier, they believed a pol-icy of arming teachers, for example, would fundamentally undermine these central priorities of teacher work. Preservice teachers already wary about the impact of school resource officers and metal detectors or other forms of surveillance on students emphasized the negative effect that an armed teacher would necessarily have on students' well-being, their willingness to enter in relationship with teachers, and their ability to learn. One teacher, who had had challenging relationships with teachers he found intimidating during his own high school expe-rience, was especially dedicated to establishing a safe space and build-ing supportive relationships with all of his students. He explained:

Something that's extremely important in teaching is building relationships with students. People who [believe in arming teachers] think of teachers more like authority, which is how law enforcement is viewed, and I think that's wrong. The teacher's job is to work through problems with students and I want students to be able to come to me with their problems and things that are challenging them and not fear me. I don't want any student to fear me. I had teachers I feared in high school and it was awful. I would never have gone to them about anything and that was probably detrimental to my education, because I didn't feel comfortable going to them.

In the context of the Teacher Protection Act in Wisconsin, teachers also felt that the policy could exacerbate feelings of distrust and fear between teachers and students. One teacher pointed to the tension between knowing about past student disciplinary records and positive interactions between teachers and students. They wondered, "How is this restorative? Best practices from teachers should be building relationships that facilitate knowledge. This background knowledge [from the reporting provisions] may actually hinder that relationship building." Another teacher questioned the utility of the type of information made available through the Teacher Protection Act in fostering relationships with students, reflecting that the policy "feels gossipy rather than helpful." In addressing the interconnected issues of discipline, access to information, trust, and the teacher–student relationship, Wisconsin teachers identified other possible approaches to improving school safety. Unlike the provisions in the proposed act, they argued in favor of policies that might, for example, support increased teacher time outside of the existing academic curriculum to relationship building between students and teachers.

Both the preservice and practicing teacher cohorts emphasized the critical importance of the teacher–student connection and viewed relationship building as a key component of their professional responsibility as teachers. They made clear their objections to any policy that would challenge those relationships, either through the absence of clear and effective guidelines or by creating an atmosphere of uncertainty and fear, thereby eroding teachers' ability to build the trusting classroom communities critical to learning.

Student Safety and Mental Health

Finally, teachers in both Wisconsin and Massachusetts had concerns about the implications of proposed and enacted school discipline and safety policies for students with mental health challenges. In Massachusetts, preservice teachers' concern about the possibility of gun violence in their sites, combined with the absence of clear school safety policies, directly impacted their pedagogical decision-making (Hara, 2020). They described being on alert for student behaviors that could be interpreted as cause for concern, with one teacher characterizing the experience as being "hyper aware at all times." One teacher shared how this hyperawareness impacted their interactions with some students, recounting:

> There are times when I'll read some of the poetry or some of the things that students are writing or saying, and it is concerning. There's already one thing where there's one student who non-stop talks about murder and blood, and that is just something that [I've made sure] the guidance counselor is aware of. . . . I don't want to be tiptoeing around a student because I'm afraid. I have had to almost check myself a little bit, because I think I have let that influence the way that I'm then reacting or then responding to that student.

The heightened alertness described in the quote above was particularly troubling for elementary-level teachers, who believed that the core responsibility of their work as teachers of young children was to nurture and support students as individuals (Hara, 2020). Teachers struggled to square that hefty responsibility with consciously or subconsciously anticipating potential violent behavior in children. An elementary teacher placed in the early grades said, "I'm supposed to be supporting human souls, you know? Not thinking, 'Could you maybe do this horrible thing?'"

In Wisconsin, too, teachers defined mental health as a significant factor in their classroom experiences and drew a direct line between student mental health status and the proposals in the Teacher Protection Act. They identified a range of supports for student mental health left unaddressed by the proposed policy. First, they argued schools need increased education, awareness, and resources for student mental health issues. Both students and teachers, they argued, need more support around social–emotional well-being and mental health as a whole. One teacher pointed out, "Teachers are not therapists, but they have to become one if there is a need." They felt the proposed legislation did nothing to address these root causes of student behaviors at school. Second, teachers highlighted the need to give students tools to deal with past traumatic experiences and challenging situations that unfold at school. Not only would such proactive efforts support students' mental health, but they would also contribute to addressing potential issues prior to escalation to a possible discipline or safety concern. Finally, given the connections between mental health and school behavior, teachers felt the proposed legislation could threaten student privacy related to their mental health by opening access to behavioral records. The legislation failed to recognize the need for a more nuanced, humanizing approach to students' behavior records prioritizing social, emotional, and mental health without threatening students' rights to privacy.

Teachers in Wisconsin and Massachusetts had significant concerns about the motivations behind and the underlying assumptions informing the design of school safety and discipline policies. They also had significant concerns about the impact of these policies on their teaching practice and their relationships with students. As teachers confronted policies that are deeply rooted in broad societal norms and longstanding racial inequities, they grappled with the question of how to advocate for policy aligned with their personal beliefs, ethics, and their professional visions.

BARRIERS TO ADVOCACY: THE PRESERVICE TEACHER PERSPECTIVE

As evidenced by the narratives in this chapter, teachers were keenly aware of the importance of policies' underlying theories of action, speaking with great nuance about their concerns with the fundamental assumptions informing the framing of the "problem" of school safety and student discipline. They pointed out the absence of clear data supporting policy design, seeking clarity on the evidence informing the range of proposed and adopted policies described in this chapter. They had specific critiques of the proposed mechanisms for implementation of the policies. Finally, teachers reflected on both the framing and potential implications of the policy on the focus popula-tions, for example, on the mental health of students and pre-existing racialized patterns in school discipline.

Across both sites, teachers also reflected on their agency and capacity for policy advocacy in this area. First, preservice teachers in Massachusetts wanted more training on how to deal with school safety in their schools, citing a silence in their training that left them ill-prepared to cope with the complexities of such a weighty issue. Preservice teachers in this group did not observe teachers in their field placements taking an active role in advocating for school policy ad-dressing potential attacks. They were not aware of practicing teachers in their schools active in policy design or advocacy related to school safety. On the whole, they had little opportunity to practice making sense of, responding to, or advocating around school safety in ap-prenticeship with an experienced teacher or a teacher educator (Hara, 2020). In fact, when one student teacher had a student in class who had repeatedly written about violent topics, she was not included in decision-making around how to address the situation. The teacher expressed mixed feelings, explaining, "Thank goodness that I am stu-dent teaching and I have someone that I can come to and say, 'OK, is this something that I need to be, like, investigating further?' . . . But personally, that was just kind of taken from me and my [supervising practitioner] was like, 'I'm going to handle it.'" Another preservice teacher expressed a similar desire for explicit guidance on how to advocate on the topic of school safety policy, saying:

> I'm still five weeks into student teaching? Six weeks in? So, I'm still learning, new situations are coming up every day that I have to adjust to. But you want to be prepared for every situation, like if students are going to fight in my classroom, or whatever, you still want to know what policy is in terms of that, what the procedural things that are in place. How should I react, and what are the ways that I could react?

Very few of the preservice teachers in the Massachusetts group asked for guidance from their supervising teachers or from their uni-versity teacher educators around any of the problems of practice de-scribed in this chapter. One preservice teacher explained, "I mentioned it to my university supervisor once. But there's so much other stuff to keep track of, and I don't really think anything would have changed, anyway." Because of the substantial requirements of teacher licensure and competing needs in the classroom, most preservice teachers in this group felt that their supervising practitioners and university supervisors had limited bandwidth to prioritize school shootings as an area of practice.

Preservice teachers' lack of self-efficacy around policy, combined with their observations of their mentor teachers, contributed to a sense of futility around challenging gun-related issues in schools (Hara, 2020). One preservice teacher stated, "I don't think there's anything that you can really do to prevent [a shooting] from happening in the school building except for gun control and limiting the number of guns and broader gun legislation. I feel strongly about that." The Massachusetts preservice teachers' own experiences growing up as students in the United States also contributed to their skepticism about the likelihood of change. One student teacher said "Most of us here have grown up hearing this stuff in the news, you know? What's going to change now? I wouldn't even know how to be the one who makes anything different on a policy level. I don't know how to do that."

HIGH-LEVERAGE STRATEGY: EDCAMPS AS TEACHER-LED PROFESSIONAL DEVELOPMENT

Though the preservice teachers quoted in the section above have reason to be skeptical about the potential for meaningful gun control, we believe teachers can be involved in school safety and discipline policy advocacy in impactful ways. We propose the model of the EdCamp as a useful strategy for increasing teacher policy advocacy around educational policies such as the ones described in this chapter.

The structure and focus of EdCamps reflect important themes from the research around supporting teacher policy advocacy centering on the idea that targeted, meaningful professional development is a key element in increasing teachers' capacity for policy action. The teachers in this chapter identified key skills and information necessary to overcoming the barriers to meaningful policy action relating to school safety and discipline policies. First, both groups called for additional professional development specifically for capacity-building around policy advocacy for preservice and practicing teachers. They saw a need for more training and opportunities for teachers to learn about the details of proposed policies, as well as the options available to them in advocacy around safety and discipline policies within their respective school buildings and beyond. The preservice teachers highlighted the importance of specific guidance around navigating a charged policy topic like school safety and the choices for action accessible to them. They called for the integration of policy advocacy into the apprenticeship model of student teaching so they might rehearse options for policy engagement for systemic change in the same way they do lesson planning and assessment.

Second, teachers called for professional development that could address root causes of bias and racism feeding some teachers' feelings of fear and a perceived need for protection from students. One teacher envisioned a model for professional learning in which teachers could "name what it means to be afraid in the classroom." As the teacher explained, by inviting teachers to elaborate on these real concerns, such a conversation could also lead to a "deep dive into possible true issues like racism." Opportunities for discussion about potentially racialized, fear-based assumptions and motivations behind a policy like the Teacher Protection Act, teachers argued, might prompt teachers to act, particularly at their local school levels.

Three characteristics of the EdCamp model align directly with what teachers suggested to be necessary conditions for teacher policy advocacy. A key component of the EdCamp approach is to create sustainable connections between teachers to enable ongoing conversation and collaboration across schools, districts, or even states. The avenue through which the Wisconsin cohort of teachers came together to discuss the Teacher Protection Act is in itself an example of the type of professional development that takes place at EdCamps and can increase teacher capacity around policy advocacy. EdCamps tend to be technology-heavy, with online, backchannel discussions via Twitter (#EdCamp) and a shared Google doc for resources and notes relating to each session. Networking may be particularly important for novice teachers such as those in the Massachusetts group described in this chapter, who had little opportunity to engage in conversation with other like-minded educators about shared policy concerns. The ability to meet with other teachers, whether virtually or in person, around topics of shared interest is one way to address the gap in the preservice teacher professional training identified by the preservice teachers in Massachusetts.

Another key element of the EdCamp model is to build knowledge while emphasizing action with the goal of extending engagement beyond the conference. Participants such as those in the Wisconsin cohort described in this chapter could collaborate on specific advocacy actions such as letter writing, network building, or communication with local policymakers and politicians. EdCamps provide a setting in which teachers can work together to move from policy discussion to policy action in their efforts to guide policy in closer alignment with their professional beliefs and visions. Teachers such as the Massachusetts preservice teachers who felt limited agency to effect change might benefit from authentic, collaborative time with peers and more experienced teachers in identifying actionable steps.

Finally, EdCamps are designed to be accessible, especially to educators. At EdCamps, participants typically propose topics in an open mic–type atmosphere and then discuss them during a series of 1-hour breakout sessions hosted by teachers that same day. Anyone can attend or host an EdCamp, and the costs are low, unlike the very high fees typically associated with other professional conferences. Preservice teachers, practicing teachers, and teacher educators can locate established EdCamps via the EdCamp Foundation (www.digitalpromise .org/edcamp). The EdCamp Foundation at Digital Promise also provides support and guidance for groups wanting to start and host their own EdCamp, on a scale ranging from events at single schools, districts, or teacher education programs to large statewide events. Whether novice or experienced, rural or urban, teachers across the country can access, attend, and create an EdCamp on the topics of their choice and with multiple engagement modalities.

CONCLUSION

The narratives in this chapter illustrate how teachers at various stages of their professional careers make meaning of policies intended to address issues of safety and discipline in schools. Preservice and practicing teachers in the two cases identified cross-cutting themes of efficacy, racism, mental health, and the teacher–student relationship as key considerations in their assessment of the safety and discipline policies in their respective sites. They called for a range of professional development options, including those that would train teachers and other education professionals to better understand mental health challenges, to challenge racist and biased practices in schooling, and to engage in mentorship for novice teachers around policy engagement as a whole.

Ultimately, the teachers in both sites wanted to know more and wanted to know how to *do* more. The discussions that emerged from their collaborative reflections demonstrate the value of a specific form of professional development: one that is teacher-driven, tailored to the issues most salient to teachers, and directed toward community and connection building.

EdCamps provide teachers access to information about enacted and proposed policies, offer teachers dedicated time and space to discuss policies in concert with like-minded peers, and bolster agency and capacity for tangible actions related to policy. They hold significant potential for teachers seeking advocacy opportunities around all policies, including those that appear as deeply entrenched as those relating to school safety. Though the discussions showcased in this chapter pertain specifically to issues of safety and discipline in schools, the critical importance of collaborative professional development led by teachers is a refrain that echoes through all of the policy contexts in this book.

DISCUSSION QUESTIONS

1. The practicing and preservice teachers in this chapter encountered a range of proposed and enacted policies relating to school safety. What options were available to teachers in response to these policies? What might have been the possible implications of taking these actions for:
   a. Teachers and their colleagues
   b. Students
   c. The effectiveness of these policies
2. Despite their desire to engage in conversation around the topic of school shootings with their students, most preservice teachers in this chapter had little opportunity to talk with practicing teachers about this area of policy. How might preservice teachers benefit from the EdCamp strategy? What needs to happen for preservice teachers to have full access to EdCamps as a resource?
3. Teachers in this chapter identified a theory of action in school safety policies that differed from their own understandings of

the teacher role and responsibility with respect to discipline, safety, and relationships with students. What advice might a practicing teacher or teacher educator give to a preservice teacher confronting a gap between what they are asked to do and what they believe they should do?

CHAPTER 2

Assessment Policy

> When I started here 12 years ago we didn't have a curriculum, it was "We trust you as teachers." Now everyone needs to be on the same page, and you need to input the data in a spreadsheet. It feels like no matter what I do, it's not good enough.
>
> —Kindergarten teacher, Massachusetts

Early each spring semester, public school classrooms from coast to coast are deep in preparation for state standardized tests. Number two pencils are sharpened, anchor charts are taken down or covered up, desks are moved into rows. Students in classrooms across the country are reminded to get a good night's sleep and to eat a healthy breakfast. The consequences of poor outcomes on tests can be serious for schools and the individuals within them; schools lose status, teachers receive public ratings based on their students' test scores, and students internalize messages about their proficiency levels and what that means about them as individuals. Whether schools depend on high test scores for prestige or for survival, the pressures are reflected in assessment policy that extends far beyond testing week itself.

Assessment policy continues to be one of the most influential factors in the nature of teachers' work. Standardized tests are only one manifestation of assessment policy, but one that is especially powerful in shaping teaching and learning. High-stakes testing is not new and has shaped instructional decision-making, teacher evaluation, and curriculum for decades, in spite of a long and problematic history in the United States and in countries around the globe.

In this chapter, we describe teachers' experiences with assessment policy in Wisconsin and in Massachusetts. We begin by contextualizing the data in a brief overview of standardized testing in the recent history of schooling in the United States and the assessment policy landscapes in both states. We then identify key themes in teachers' experiences in both contexts. Practicing and preservice teachers experienced assessment policy as critically impactful to their instruction and to teacher and student well-being, among a myriad of other aspects of life in schools. They shared deeply rooted concerns about the impact of testing on the nature of teaching and learning, as well as about the implementation of assessment policies in their respective schools.

Unsurprisingly, the role of COVID-19 in teachers' views about assessment policy advocacy is a significant thread in this chapter. The story of standardized testing during the pandemic is a complex one. Most states suspended assessments in spring 2020, while others made them optional in the 2020–2021 school year. As a result, fewer tests were administered nationwide and the quality of the resulting data as a measure of student learning was limited at best. The states and districts that opted to administer some form of standardized assessment in later stages of the pandemic sought not only to assess student learning, but also to gauge how much students were falling behind because of pandemic "learning loss," and to track the gaps in learning experienced due to unequal access to virtual or hybrid classes. Local, school-based assessments followed a similar pattern. As the narratives you will read in this chapter illustrate, the push to measure student learning persisted even in the midst of a global crisis, and in some cases was amplified by the fear of falling "behind." The evolution of assessment policy during the COVID-19 crisis further amplified and complicated teachers' existing concerns. It is in the context of the longstanding influence of standardized testing and the added, intense pressure from the pandemic that we examine teachers' experiences with assessment policy and their advocacy in this area.

Teachers' motivation to advocate against aggressive reliance on standardized test data in policy decision-making increased as a result of their experiences with pandemic teaching. In addition, they desired greater capacity and advocacy power around assessment policy. In this chapter, we propose collaborative mentorship as a strategy that has the potential to respond to this need. In this model, practicing and preservice teachers engage in a structured approach to identifying, analyzing, and potentially participating in advocacy around specific educational policies they deem most relevant in their day-to-day work. Though mentoring often implies a relationship in which a more experienced teacher shares knowledge and skills with a novice teacher, collaborative mentorship is multidirectional, with practicing teachers and preservice teachers learning from one another through critical dialogue (Ellis et al., 2020; Lopez, 2013). We have found this type of collaborative, multidirectional mentorship helps both experienced and preservice teachers in their sensemaking around policy advocacy.

We describe how teachers in two states used the framework of collaborative mentorship to discuss policy advocacy relating to assessment before and during the COVID-19 pandemic. We weave throughout these findings vignettes from collaborative mentorship dyads in Massachusetts. These excerpts demonstrate how collaborative mentorship can support preservice and practicing teachers as they learn together and build tools and habits toward action. Later in the chapter, we offer a blueprint, albeit a flexible one, for initiating collaborative mentorship models drawing on our learnings from our work with teachers in our sample. We argue that structured collaborative mentorship provides teachers at all career stages important space to identify and discuss policy that matters to them, to think in community about their roles with respect to these policies, and to envision ways of taking collective action for change.

STANDARDIZED ASSESSMENTS AND EDUCATION POLICY

Standardized assessments are tests intended to be taken by large numbers of students under consistent conditions and graded in a consistent way (Lynch, 2016). They are often used to gauge students' academic performance and needs in specific areas (e.g., math, reading, writing). As already noted, they are used widely to inform policy decisions at federal, state, and local levels, and as such hold significant symbolic and tangible power. One need only listen to the evening news or read the headlines during test-taking season to witness how central standardized tests have become to public perceptions of school success or failure. High scores on state standardized tests are lauded as evidence of academic rigor and highly effective teaching, while persistently low test scores are used as evidence of bad teachers and bad schools. The implications of such policy framing are far-reaching; when student performance on standardized assessments is labeled as failing, so too are public school systems and those that work in them. Public discourse around disparities in test scores between racial, ethnic, and socioeconomic student subgroups frequently ignores root causes such as lack of resources, inequitable school funding formulas, and inequitable access to healthcare. Educational policy designed on the premise that low test scores are a result of insufficient skill, effort, or commitment on the part of teachers results in punishments for educators and schools when scores fail to improve.

The emphasis on high-stakes testing trickles down to other forms of assessment policy. Teachers across the country have long reported an increase in district and building-level standardized assessments designed to track student performance over the course of the academic year. The ubiquity of these assessments and their relationship to high-stakes state testing have a powerful impact on teachers' freedom to make curricular and instructional choices, or to instantiate alternative understandings of student learning.

Teachers feel a responsibility to prepare their students for assessments that are necessary to their long-term educational success. At the same time, they are acutely aware of the negative impacts of current trends in assessment policy on students, teachers, and schools. Motivated by these concerns, teachers nationwide have engaged in advocacy in this area, pushing back against burdensome high-stakes tests by organizing walkouts and testing boycotts. Similarly, parent and student groups have organized in opposition to standardized testing, most notably in the Opt-Out Movement and other efforts to inform families about their rights with respect to high-stakes testing. Despite these efforts, standardized testing remains a reality for the majority of students and teachers in the United States at this time, one with powerful impacts on teaching and learning.

TEACHERS AND ASSESSMENT POLICY BEFORE COVID-19

The teachers in both states reported longstanding questions and concerns about the reliance on standardized testing in their districts and schools. Their primary focus was on the value placed on scores on high-stakes state tests, but also included the use of data from those assessments and the growing number of in-house assessments intended to monitor student progress. The vignettes below illustrate how participating teachers in two collaborative mentorship dyads in Massachusetts made sense of assessment policy in their respective schools.

"How Is This a Good Measure?"

Kate and Daria were partners in an elementary grade practicing/preservice teacher dyad in Massachusetts who selected assessment policy as a central focus of discussion in their collaborative mentorship dyad. In one of their collaborative memos, they took turns describing their views on the implementation of assessment policy in their elementary school in the late winter of 2020. Specifically, they focused on the example of a district-mandated math assessment for which their administration had implemented a policy limiting the type of preparation permitted to students and teachers. They wrote paragraph after paragraph, offering insight into the nature of the policy in their site and its impact on their teaching and their students' learning.

Kate, the practicing teacher in the 2nd-grade classroom, described the policy as follows: "We were told that we could not give review questions that mirror the test questions, we needed to cover any math visual in our classroom, and we could only give the assessment in two sessions." She objected to the gap between the policy's directives and what she believed to be sound practice. Daria, the student teacher, worried about the differences between test day conditions and learning conditions in the day-to-day practice of her math classroom. Kate agreed, pointing out that teachers, and therefore students, had not been informed of the policy and its limitations until preparation for the assessment was largely complete. She wrote, "We were told this two days before we needed to start giving the assessment. I would not have taught students to use the visual supports in the room if I had known this policy." Kate's comments highlight a recurring theme of teachers often feeling shut out of policy decisions directly impacting teaching and learning.

Daria went on to highlight the tension she perceived between fidelity to test-taking policy and prioritization of her students' academic success. She wrote:

> As an educator, I want my students to be successful when taking benchmark assessments and/or any classroom tests. The recent change to the test taking policy made it difficult to provide students with the same resources that they had been using in our classroom. As an educator, I felt as though these students were being set up to fail our recent math assessment.

On her part, Kate questioned the validity of data derived from an assessment for which teachers have limited opportunity to prepare and students receive insufficient support. She wrote, "This data is used to determine which students need math intervention support. If the data is not accurate then all of these things will be affected." In addition to feeling frustrated about not being kept in the loop about assessment policy implementation, the two teachers had substantive concerns about the impact on students' test performance. Kate and Daria wondered together about the power and influence built into standardized test data, its actual utility for sound pedagogical decision-making, and the negative impacts of poor fit between assessment and intervention.

Concerns About Data-Driven Decision-Making

In addition to questions about the match between assessment policy and good educational decision-making, teachers had concerns about their own self-efficacy relating to effective use of standardized assessment data. Betsy and Hannah were partners in a Kindergarten dyad in Massachusetts who also selected assessment policy as a key area of focus in their collaborative discussions about policy. Their exchanges held evidence of how their sense of professional obligation to comply with district and school assessment policy often rubbed up against their deep commitment to developmentally appropriate, play-based instruction for their students. Hannah, an experienced early childhood educator, described the problems inherent in excess standardized assessment of any kind for young children. Betsy, the student teacher, agreed, writing, "This is kindergarten!"

In one of their reflective memos, Betsy and Hannah focused on teacher capacity to prepare for, implement, and interpret high-stakes standardized assessments. Hannah raised the topic of teachers' limited capacity around analyzing data for practical use. Having witnessed how her school used assessment as a key driver of pedagogical decision-making, Hannah was troubled by her own lack of self-confidence in effective application of test data to her teaching practice. She wrote, "It's frustrating when given assessments and not being trained to adequately administer and interpret the data to direct and adjust teaching practices." She reported having received limited training in her early childhood teacher education program around high-stakes test-driven instructional decision-making. She attributed this in part to the disconnect between standardized testing and the developmental needs of 4- and 5-year-old children.

Betsy, the preservice teacher, also expressed doubt about the meaningful application of assessment data to pedagogical decision-making. She saw little evidence that administrators or teachers were using data to improve instruction. As a result, she questioned the utility of collecting so much data, especially given the drawbacks of doing so in the early grades. She explained:

> After results from some of the standardized–schoolwide or grade level–testing have been released, it doesn't seem like the results are being used. For example, the teachers seem confused on how to interpret the results and are not given the opportunity to adjust instruction accordingly. This makes the standardized testing seem meaningless.

Both Betsy and Hannah were inclined to adhere to district and school directives relating to assessment policy. They believed that a good faith effort toward fidelity to policy was part of their job, and they recognized that students would need to display evidence of achievement in order to advance in their academic careers. However, like all teachers, they also wanted to feel that testing could enhance their students' progress and therefore wanted to be equipped to use assessment data to their students' benefit. In the absence of professional training directly targeting data-driven decision-making, though, they objected to administering stressful, time-consuming standardized tests to young children with no guarantee of improvement in teaching and learning.

Teachers in Wisconsin, too, were worried about the ongoing impact of assessment policy on curriculum and instruction. Whereas the teachers in Massachusetts raised the issue of data not being used effectively, teachers in Wisconsin underscored the problems inherent in relying too much on any one source of data to drive instructional practice. In their collaborative conversations, teachers in different Wisconsin districts commiserated about the push toward "data-driven decision-making" that relied almost exclusively on standardized test scores. One teacher described the data conversation in classrooms and schools as having become "just about achievement, and just measured by tests."

Wisconsin teachers also noted that the emphasis on standardized test data as the primary driver for instructional decision-making seemed to grow each year. One stated, "I wish we had other ways to show growth besides standardized test scores. If we want learning to be differentiated, then the assessments need to [be differentiated]. We were doing these [learning] goals beforehand but didn't need to track and have artifacts to prove it."

Above all, the teachers in our groups were worried about the impact of assessment policy on their students' well-being. One Wisconsin teacher described how tests increased anxiety and triggered explosive behaviors in students in her special education classes. Many teachers expressed worry about the pressure of high-stakes tests on student mental health, while others were concerned about the lasting impact of the pressure of data-driven assessment policy on student–teacher relationships. One Wisconsin teacher lamented, "[Teachers] are so pressured to look at the data that they forget to look at their kids." Teachers who were already reluctant to champion assessments in which they had little confidence of efficacy or applicability to instructional improvement were particularly unwilling to do so given their concerns about student well-being.

Teachers as Policy Targets

Discussions of assessment policy in education often focus individually on the K–12, teacher education, or teacher workforce levels. However, our conversations with preservice and practicing teachers evidenced the importance of looking more broadly at how assessment policy plays out simultaneously across all three groups: students, preservice teachers, and practicing teachers. Indeed, preservice and practicing teachers, like their students, are acted upon as targets of assessment policy.

Because of their liminal position across the K–12 and teacher education spaces, preservice candidates are uniquely positioned to speak to the multiple implications of assessment policy for educators. Preservice teachers are subject to assessment policy in a variety of ways over the course of their professional formation. They must pass their own set of high-stakes assessments in the form of teacher licensure tests, and must also successfully complete the battery of state-mandated teacher preparedness assessments administered over the course of their teacher education coursework and student teaching practicum experiences.

There is robust evidence of the problems around standardized, high-stakes teacher testing. In addition to the inherent bias of all standardized tests (Au, 2009), teacher tests may especially contribute to inequality because they are often used as gatekeepers to teacher education programs. Unlike in other professional fields, successful completion of teacher tests is in many undergraduate teacher education programs a prerequisite for entry to coursework (Petchauer, 2012), contributing to the ongoing exclusion of historically underrepresented groups in education. At the same time, those who support teacher testing champion it as a means of bolstering achievement by ensuring that each student will have a qualified teacher (Barber & Mourshed, 2007). Other proponents contend that demanding certification requirements will increase the number of skillful teachers, thereby raising the status of the profession and attracting stronger candidates (Fernández, 2018). Today, licensure tests remain typical in teacher education (Nettles et al., 2011), with some 40 states requiring at least one test for initial teacher licensure (Petchauer, 2012).

The push for teacher assessment does not stop at initial licensure. Practicing teachers, too, are targets of high-stakes assessment policies. Teachers across the country are subject to a range of evaluation systems that vary in scope and intensity. For example, like many other states, Wisconsin has a set of policies in state statute and administrative law around reviewing educator effectiveness. Teachers set student learning objectives (SLOs) each year, for which they are expected to use standardized assessments to measure growth, and that are used as part of principals' evaluations.

Teachers in Wisconsin described making sense of assessment policy targeting practicing teachers in much the same way they did with assessment policy targeting their students. One group of teachers talked about ways to manage and work within the requirement, effectively making and remaking SLO policy as they implemented it in their respective classrooms. For example, one teacher suggested writing learning objectives in more general terms, like measuring growth on a "district-wide assessment" versus on the "reading section of the Measures of Academic Progress (MAP) test." Another teacher proposed setting SLOs for a small group of targeted students rather than an entire class and setting the goal for growth on assessments at 85% rather than 100%.

Teachers were aware of the problems with SLO policy's underlying assumptions and with their implementation. They did their best to interpret and remake policy in ways that made the most sense for their individual situations and contexts, creating SLO policy that they believed better served their students' needs as well as their own while remaining in compliance with policy texts. In so doing, they also skillfully maneuvered the nuances of implementing assessment policy that impacted their own performance evaluations as well as the learning experiences of their students.

Constraints on Policy Advocacy

Despite their constant exposure to and expertise with assessment policy, teachers in both states described their agency in this policy area as limited to their individual classrooms. In Massachusetts, one practicing teacher shared an example of how she and a group of her colleagues reacted to a last-minute notification of a policy change from her school administrative team. She explained:

> A few teachers were together on Saturday when we received [an email about an assessment policy change] and we all were upset, and complained, and wondered where it came from. That is as far as our advocacy went. Many other teachers complained to each other, but no one spoke up or asked where it came from.

Preservice teachers in Massachusetts referenced their limited professional training as a constraint on their capacity for policy advocacy. One wrote, "At this point, working as a student teacher, I don't feel confident enough to make a change to a school or district wide policy." She went on to describe an example of how she might work within a school building assessment policy around the types of supports permitted on a math test, saying: "Moving forward, I will encourage students to use resources like an open number line or a hundreds chart more often, since these are allowed on benchmark math assessments." For this student, as for many of her peers, it was more realistic to work with the policy than to advocate for change.

Many preservice teachers felt that they were getting on-the-job insight into the pressing need for policy advocacy in assessment, if not training in how to advocate for or against specific policies. However, they grappled with balancing their desire for training around navigating assessment policy in their K–12 sites under conditions of pervasive assessment and accountability discourse in the field of teacher education itself. In one example, preservice teachers in Massachusetts pointed to the intense pressure they felt to pass teacher licensure tests, a pressure that was felt acutely by candidates in licensure areas that required three or more high-stakes tests to be completed. They wondered how teacher education programs could effectively equip teachers to be advocates for or against K–12 assessment policy while simultaneously requiring them to comply with teacher education high-stakes assessments as a condition for licensure.

Preservice teachers interpreted the compliance required in their teacher education programs as being at odds with policy advocacy. They described ongoing messaging from administrators in their teacher education programs encouraging preservice teachers to be cautious and compliant in their roles as apprentices. Though they recognized that this message was directed toward their role in their practicum placements, they nevertheless internalized it in other areas of their training. One preservice teacher in Massachusetts shared, "In a lot of our training they always say, if you fail [student teaching] you fail the program, so behave yourself. At least from where I am now, I'm mostly implementing policy and behaving myself."

The pressure to comply was closely entwined with preservice teachers' status as job candidates. Student teachers believed they needed to consider how advocacy might be perceived by potential employers. Given the requirements of program completion and the uncertainty of their future employment, preservice teachers grappled with wanting to be agentic in their interactions with educational policy that mattered to them and worrying that doing so would make them less desirable as a job candidate. Many preservice teachers identified a critical need for teacher education programs and the individuals within them to name the siren song of assessment and accountability. They wanted authentic and meaningful opportunities for apprenticeship in how to navigate the realities of high-stakes assessment in K–12 and teacher education.

Preservice teachers are not alone in facing challenges to advocacy relating to assessment policy. Independent of employment status, the climate within a school building is a major factor in whether any teacher feels comfortable advocating beyond closed doors. And, even when a school climate is conducive to teacher policy voice, organizational and structural choices can still circumvent advocacy. In their collaborative mentorship dyad, Kate and Daria discussed examples of supports and impediments for teacher policy advocacy within a school building. Kate, the practicing teacher, shared:

I feel very comfortable voicing my opinion when the discussion is brought up, but so far our principal has not brought it up to us. . . . In past years we have had a time in our faculty meeting where we could bring any issues to the principal's attention and then everyone would have a chance to weigh in on that subject. Currently our principal does not include a time for open discussion. It is difficult to discuss a policy when there is no time set aside to discuss policy.

Wisconsin teachers, too, identified finding time and space for advocacy as a major roadblock to consistent advocacy. One teacher reflected, "At our school we talk at lunch and we talk about [state tests]. We talk when we are at [political] rallies, but we can't encourage people to do that [while in school]. And we don't have a lot of time to sit and talk as a staff because it is so go-go-go."

Teachers were well aware that even in the increasingly time-constrained context of K–12 public schools, administrators have some say over how school time is used. Teachers saw room for administrators to make intentional choices in schedules, action lists, and professional development sessions prioritizing teacher engagement in policy. Still, most teachers in our groups were less than optimistic about the likelihood of their principals doing so in a sustained way.

Ultimately, preservice and practicing teachers in both states wanted to know more about how to advocate for or against different assessment policies, and they wanted opportunities to discuss options with teachers in their own communities and contexts. Teachers were aware of ongoing efforts among educators to advocate for changes in assessment policy on a national level and wondered about how to make change happen in their own towns. A practicing teacher in Wisconsin wondered aloud, "What would happen if [teachers in] all districts said we are not taking [state test]? How do you mobilize around that?"

TEACHERS AND ASSESSMENT POLICY DURING COVID-19

As in all other areas of educational policy, the COVID-19 pandemic shifted the high-stakes assessment landscape in fundamental ways. When schools closed, it was evident that states had no choice but to cancel high-stakes tests for the academic year. The pressure relating to standardized tests, typically at a boiling point by the spring, was eclipsed by the immediate demands of the pandemic. Safety, well-being, and basic access to instruction necessarily took precedence, and the push to assess student learning was momentarily halted. While official policy texts pertaining to assessment were not permanently revised, many states implemented temporary changes that effectively froze standardized testing. This move was paralleled in teacher education, where many states had no choice but to lift requirements for teacher tests to be passed as gateways to licensure in the face of school and testing site closures.

This policy shift would otherwise have been difficult to imagine. In addition to being deeply ingrained in the culture of schooling, testing is a colossal industry. The Brookings Institution's 2012 data estimated expenditures of $1.7 billion on standardized testing regimens (Chingos, 2012). In 25 states, multimillion-dollar contracts with testing vendors represented $669 million across 45 states at the elementary level alone. Notably, in the United States, six vendors represented the bulk of those costs (Ujifusa, 2012). Testing revenue draws not only from the standardized tests themselves, but from training materials, remedial materials for students who do not meet testing benchmarks, and a host of ancillary costs. The scale of the testing industry and its financial value are staggering. Nevertheless, the pandemic resulted in a virtual elimination of high-stakes testing in education in the spring of 2020.

Ongoing Pressure of Assessment From Multiple Sources

Following the cancellation of 2020 high-stakes state testing, teachers described official messaging around assessment and accountability as subdued. That spring, districts, schools, and the individuals within them were understandably focused on issues of safety, student well-being, and access to basic instruction. Still, teachers reported that although testing was halted, the pull of accountability persisted. The drive to monitor indicators of student learning remained powerful even during the period of virtual learning. Teachers received persistent messaging pushing for assessment of student task completion and attainment of grade-level standards. Of course, teachers acknowledged that equity concerns, especially for the most vulnerable students, demanded close attention to student learning. They recognized that collecting assessment data provided necessary information about how historically marginalized students were faring in access and instruction.

However, teachers suspected that district-level motivations for measuring student learning were primarily motivated by pre-COVID-19 accountability discourse around so-called academic rigor. Even without high-stakes state tests on the schedule, teachers felt pressure to prepare students for *future* tests. Susan is a middle school teacher in a rapidly racially diversifying district in Massachusetts. She has many years of experience in both public and religious schools, and identifies pressure from administrators related to test scores as one of the largest affecting her professional life. She said, "I keep seeing these different memes on education websites about how people talk about [the state standardized tests] and that's what's needed to make students successful. But I guess not, teachers are working even harder without the fear of the [state test]."

By May of 2020, teachers were already observing a return to previous district priorities around measurements of student learning even during the very challenging phase of remote instruction. One Massachusetts middle school teacher described what they viewed as a mismatch between the realities of virtual learning for students and teachers and the ongoing pressure from district administration, saying:

> In our district we tend to work under very high standards and we're always pushing to do more all the time. Even in this situation, even when we hear from the students "I can't keep up with all the scheduling," and on our end we're only asking you to work on each class 20 minutes, and they're only in zoom meetings maybe an hour and a half, and yet we're still hearing "Don't let up too much."

Massachusetts teachers identified differences in how various stakeholders viewed assessment at this stage of pandemic instruction. They saw the push to continue measuring student learning as coming from different sources, noting a difference between school and district discourse around instruction. A middle school teacher noted, "On the one hand, our principal is saying 'It's OK, you can lower your standards a little and take it easy,' but the superintendent is still driving. Still driving the train. That worries me as we go back to school. How are we going to keep this up?" Teachers had to navigate the dual, and sometimes competing, messages from administrators both inside and beyond their school buildings.

Teachers also spoke to the role of parents in ongoing pressures relating to student achievement measures, particularly relating to notions of standards, quality instruction, and excellence. One teacher, who worked in an affluent suburb, stated:

> I know that for my district it's mostly the parents driving it. For high school we had to change how much we could give for homework and we had to give more or change how many hours because the parents are really concerned and feeling that they're not getting enough learning, and I guess not "being successful" for the next year. In our department we had to go through the standards and figure out which ones we didn't hit with our students.

Many teachers echoed the perspective that family input was increasingly at the center of assessment policy decision-making. A group of Wisconsin teachers at an EdCamp expressed concern for the ways in which parents might be increasingly involved in instructional decisions. For example, they discussed a bill that had recently been proposed in Indiana (Senate Bill 167/House Bill 1134) mandating teachers to submit lesson plans a year in advance for parental approval. As one teacher said, "If this bill comes to Wisconsin, I'm out." Teachers felt tension between truly wanting parents to be engaged in their students' school experience, but not wanting parents to have more control over curricular and instructional decisions than teachers as professional educators. One teacher lamented, "[Teaching] used to be considered an honorable profession like firefighters but now it is like we are the enemy. Parents don't see us staying at school until 5:30pm or [at this EdCamp] today. It's honestly going through my head if I should cut my line and go corporate." Teachers felt varying degrees of pressure from multiple sources in the face of worries about so-called learning loss, significant equity concerns about historically marginalized student groups, and the continual push for academic "rigor."

Conditions for Advocacy

By the fall of 2021, more than 18 months into the pandemic, all of the Massachusetts teachers were fully back in the classroom. Looking back at the previous stages of pandemic teaching, including remote instruction and the hybrid 2020–2021 academic year, teachers noted pendulum swings in their respective district and school administrators' messaging around assessment. But by the fourth semester under pandemic conditions, teachers reported an actual increase in assessments intended to gauge students' academic status after remote instruction. One kindergarten teacher reported:

> We have a very tight schedule this year, the schedules were created for us, and we have no playtime. So, in my Kindergarten class we have two recesses but we have no free choice, no play. We do math, reading, writing, social studies, and phonics every day. All of our professional practice goals this year are about assessment in our new curriculum. I feel like all I do all day is pull kids to my table for assessments.

The teacher's quote above illustrates how far-reaching assessment policy can be. To mandate the collection of assessment data in the early years, even without high stakes, necessarily has a ripple effect on teaching and learning. Unintended consequences such as the loss of free-choice time in Kindergarten have substantial implications for the experiences of 5- and 6-year-old learners.

Teacher narratives indicated that there were often multiple motivations driving assessment policy at this time. Assessment-related pressure regained momentum in affluent schools with traditionally high test scores in response to pressures to prove continued "rigor" and "achievement," where multiple Massachusetts teachers interpreted ramped-up curricular and instructional policies as evidence of school and district efforts to "get back on track." At the same time, teachers in under-resourced schools with lower test scores felt pressure to bolster assessments to measure so-called learning loss and impacts to the achievement gap. A kindergarten teacher said, "It feels like they're pushing them even more because they know they're behind and they're trying to make up for lost time. . . . We're doing so much testing."

Teachers were especially troubled by the impact of assessment tests with which students were having limited success, given the ongoing stressors of daily life with COVID. One Massachusetts teacher said, "I'm like, let me teach them. Give me a moment. They're not succeeding on these assessments." Others echoed the disconnect between their observations of students' needs and the full-court press toward additional assessments. A kindergarten teacher questioned how much state and district administrators understood about the impact of the pandemic on her students' development, saying:

> Just last week my kids started being able to look each other in the eye during morning meeting. It took months. Our curriculum doesn't really match up with where our students are emotionally. This year, it's like 'Ok, academically we're back to normal!' But we're not back to normal. The expectation and . . . the assessments are back to where they were pre-Covid but life is not back to where it was pre-Covid. My students have zero memories of life before Covid.

As evidenced earlier in this chapter, teachers in both groups had felt deep concern about the trajectory of assessment policy long before COVID-19. However, by the fall of 2021, Massachusetts teachers' objections to assessment policy and its impact on teaching, learning, and their students' social-emotional well-being were amplified by their concerns about their students' mental and social-emotional health amid the ongoing fallout of the pandemic. Teachers saw how students of all ages were suffering the consequences of loss, fear, stress, food insecurity, and isolation. The magnitude of the pandemic's impact on schools, teachers, and students ignited a new urgency around advocating for change in assessment policy.

Massachusetts teachers specifically attributed the increase in their willingness to advocate around assessment policy to their experiences teaching during COVID-19. Specifically, they described a greater likelihood and willingness to challenge the application of standardized test data to instructional and curricular decision-making in their schools and classrooms. Teachers who had long felt uneasy about the prevalence and power of high-stakes standardized tests but had not spoken up before felt compelled to do so. As one teacher put it, "This is a bridge too far. What have we learned from the last two years?"

Teachers identified an important shift in how they viewed their sphere of influence and responsibility around assessment policy. Those whose engagement prior to COVID-19 had been limited to private or team-level conversations expanded their scope to school-wide meetings. They witnessed this in their peers as well. A teacher explained:

We had a professional development day where there was some push back like 'What are we doing with this?' and also 'Don't forget we're still not back to 100% normal.' I do feel that the administration team is hearing that from teachers. We're saying, 'We're not going to go full speed ahead with data analysis this year.'

Teachers described being motivated by the pandemic to advocate for a reimagined approach to assessment policy in their schools, something they did not do prior to the public health crisis. Still, aware of broader teacher movements relating to assessment policy in other parts of the country, teachers in our groups recognized that their advocacy did not yet extend beyond their respective school buildings. Nevertheless, their experiences during COVID-19 increased their interest in finding ways to increase their capacity for advocacy in this tremendously impactful policy area.

HIGH-LEVERAGE STRATEGY: COLLABORATIVE MENTORSHIP

In this chapter, we identify collaborative mentorship as a means of supporting teachers as they explore the potential for policy advocacy. There are multiple ways of defining mentorship in teaching. Some focus on the relationship between mentor and mentee (Kram, 1985), while others emphasize the process (Smith, 2007) or the context in which the mentoring takes place (Fairbanks et al., 2000). Most approaches imply a hierarchical relationship in which individuals have different levels of experience and access to resources of capital and power, and in which mentoring is particularly beneficial in enhancing new teachers' learning (Feiman-Nemser, 2003). However, other explorations of mentorship have illustrated the mutual benefits of mentorship for both parties (Hall et al., 2008). Though most analyses of mentorship in education focus on the development of so-called pedagogical skills, which traditionally omit policy work, we apply the concept here to the development of policy advocacy skills as a key component of teacher practice.

Mentorship differs from supervision in that it centers on supporting growth and providing feedback without judgment or evaluation (Ambrosetti & Dekkers, 2010), which may be of particular importance when discussing policy issues. Ironically, for the teachers in this chapter, judgment-free mentorship was facilitated in the supervising teacher–student teacher context because policy knowledge and advocacy are not components of teacher education assessments or teacher evaluations. Had practicing teachers been responsible for assessing their students' progress toward policy knowledge, free, reciprocal exploration of the policy views and practice may have been more challenging.

The Massachusetts and Wisconsin cases illustrate two different examples of collaborative mentorship. In both cases, the mentorship models were guided by three questions: (1) what do preservice and practicing teachers know about policy advocacy? (2) how do they assess their self-efficacy for policy advocacy? and (3) how does this change, if at all, after a semester-long collaborative exploration of policy advocacy? As demonstrated by the data in this chapter, assessment policy emerged as a central theme for teachers in both states, with preservice and practicing teachers choosing to focus workshop discussions and reflective memo discussions on the specifics of testing and accountability in their respective schools.

In Massachusetts, pairs of practicing and preservice teachers partnered to take part in two workshops on the foundations of policy advocacy. All pairs were composed of a supervising practitioner and a student teacher placed in their classroom for the duration of an academic semester. The first workshop took place at the start of the student teaching practicum, and the final workshop took place at the end of the semester. In between the workshops, partners engaged in structured discussions on policy topics they identified as most salient to their practice. After each discussion, they cowrote and submitted reflection notes sharing their individual and collective understandings of policy in their classrooms and schools. Each subsequent reflective memo asked dyads to consider any change in their thinking in the time that had elapsed. Though the pairings were initially intended to last only the duration of the student teaching semester, we followed up with participants again over a year into the COVID-19 pandemic.

In Wisconsin, groups of about 30 preservice teachers took part in two 2-hour workshops on the foundations of policy advocacy. The workshops were designed by teacher educators in consultation with practicing teachers, who then all cofacilitated the sessions together. The practicing teachers shared examples from their own classrooms and experiences to illustrate policy concepts, and then facilitated small-group discussions with the preservice teachers where they reflected

together and worked on action plans based on a policy issue of interest. In between the workshops, preservice teachers wrote reflections
in journals and worked on their action plans.

As a strategy, collaborative mentorship shows promise in responding to many of the needs identified by the teachers in this chapter.
First, teachers cited the desire to talk with peers about policy topics
impacting their daily practice in schools. Collaborative mentorship
offers an opportunity for teachers who would otherwise have no im-
petus to come together to discuss and share ideas and resources. In
both the Massachusetts and Wisconsin cases, teachers from different
backgrounds and licensure areas engaged in workshops during which
they were able to talk with others about policy issues of their choice.

Second, collaborative mentorship designates a structure through
which to engage in on-the-job, professional development in action.
Teachers in our groups cited their lack of training as a significant
obstacle to action. Semester-long collaborative mentorship is no
substitute for formal coursework in teacher education programs or
sustained and intensive training. However, in the absence of policy
advocacy as a curricular focus in teacher education or in continuing
professional formation, collaborative mentorship models can provide
teachers with practical professional development relating to policy
within an organized protocol and time frame.

The perennial problem of teachers' severely limited time as an
obstacle to policy engagement is not addressed by this model. In
fact, collaborative mentorship could require teachers to take additional time out of their schedule to participate. We also recognize
some teachers we worked with came from relatively well-resourced
districts, which tend to have greater ability to provide more time to
teachers for professional learning and mentorship. Yet, we envision
the possibility of collaborative mentorship dyads taking place as part
of routinely scheduled professional development time mandated by
any school and/or district. Doing so has two benefits: first, it mitigates
the added demand on teachers' time, and second, it represents district
and school administrators' commitment to teacher policy advocacy.
An investment in a formalized model dedicated to policies that are
important to teachers creates a symbolically and materially important opportunity for teachers to practice policy work as part of their
professional responsibilities.

We believe the strategy works best when teachers are able to adapt
it to their respective contexts, constraints, and goals. The vignette below

illustrates one preservice and practicing teacher dyad's early forays into discussing a topic of interest to them: how to advocate beyond the confines of their individual roles and local contexts. Monica was a White, female student teacher in a suburban, affluent middle school in which Lisa was her supervising practitioner. Lisa is White, married to another teacher in the district, and a veteran teacher. She identified strongly as an engaged and active leader in her school. The following conversation took place early in their partnership, shortly after Monica began her practicum experience in Lisa's Spanish classroom.

> *Monica:* Even in my class that was specific to methods, my professor told us things and said "This is from the state, I can't do anything about it." It was interesting to see someone who was a department head saying "This is how it is, this is how you pass the program." I don't know where my place is.
>
> *Lisa:* I think at least in terms of effecting change in the classroom you'll have an opportunity to do that this semester. And hopefully you'll see that you have a little more influence than you have had in the past. The advantages of advocating for something you feel passionately about is that you get the change and get what you feel is more fair or right or whatever out of that. Disadvantages are the risks, I guess. It's really hard to effect change even at the building level before you have professional status. When I came in I was basically told we are so happy to have you, there's a shortage of language teachers. I guess I was vulnerable, but I felt pretty secure even as a first-year teacher. But now I have watched teachers get cut after a year.

The snapshot above shows two teachers at different stages of their careers in conversation around a topic to which they bring distinct perspectives. The student teacher begins by describing her experience in teacher education, in which she names the powerful pull of compliance exerted not only upon students, but upon those in positions of authority in teacher education. The practicing teacher, for her part, contextualizes the reality of compliance in her own school context, speaking honestly about the disadvantages and advantages of advocacy but also sharing her view that effecting change is possible.

The collaborative mentorship models as we implemented them in Wisconsin and Massachusetts yield insight that can generate more effective future iterations of this strategy. For example, the two teachers in the dyad described above were paired within the same district and within the same building. However, teachers in our groups described wanting to take action beyond their individual schools. Deliberately structuring collaborative mentorship dyads to pair teachers from different school buildings to share ideas and develop networks, or to have dynamic pairs in which preservice and practicing teacher dyads periodically pair with dyads from other schools, might be beneficial to expanding policy advocacy on a district or state scale. The ability to compare notes, find commonalities across policy contexts, and join forces could provide necessary power to teachers' policy advocacy efforts.

CONCLUSION

The narratives in this chapter illustrate how preservice and practicing teachers in two states made sense of assessment policy before and during the COVID-19 pandemic. The data indicates that while teachers had long been concerned about the connections between high-stakes accountability policy, educational equity, and academic rigor, their concerns were heightened in the pandemic period. The impact of COVID-19 was a complicating force on assessment policy's scope and influence. Teachers in Massachusetts and Wisconsin identified greater urgency around teacher advocacy relating to assessment policy as a direct outcome of the pandemic. Those practicing teachers who felt compelled to speak up against the use of standardized test data to drive decision-making power focused their advocacy within their school buildings in new ways. Both practicing and preservice teachers were uncertain about viable pathways for advocacy beyond their local settings.

Given the experiences and needs of the teachers we worked with, we argue that collaborative mentorship is a strategy that has promise for supporting teachers' desire for community, focus, and greater capacity to scale policy advocacy beyond their own schools. Collaborative mentorship models provide teachers with structure, a dedicated time and space to discuss policy, and thought partners with whom to consider the possibility of tangible actions related to policy.

The potential for gathering forces for action beyond the individual school level is especially compelling given the experiences of teachers in our groups. Though this chapter focuses specifically on assessment policy, the data from Massachusetts and Wisconsin suggest that the model has significant promise for teachers seeking advocacy opportunities in multiple policy areas.

DISCUSSION QUESTIONS

1. The narratives in this chapter suggest that many teachers felt they had little control over assessment policy in the pre-COVID era. What are tangible actions that school administrators can take in schools to increase teachers' input into assessment policy design and evaluation? What other levers might teachers have control over when it comes to assessment policy?

2. Preservice teachers in this chapter saw a gap in their training relating to assessment policy advocacy. Can teacher educators address the tension between the pull of accountability in the field of teacher education and the need to prepare teachers to successfully navigate the assessment policy landscape? What are the major resources and obstacles to this work?

3. The strategy in focus in this chapter centers on professional development through collaborative mentorship. Considering your role and context, what policy priorities would you want to address in a collaborative mentorship dyad? What parameters of the collaborative mentorship partnership (partner's role, level of experience, school/district) would be most beneficial to your priorities and needs?

CHAPTER 3

Public Health and COVID-19 Policy

Now I feel like I hang on to these briefings every time something comes
on the news. I literally recorded the eleven o'clock news because I didn't
hear all the details of the reopening plan. I feel like so many things about
our lives and how we do our jobs are hanging in the balance on these
minute-to-minute policies that are being decided.

—Practicing teacher, Massachusetts

School and public health are inextricably linked. The relationship is
multidirectional; community and public health impact the implementation and outcomes of schooling, and, given the lack of universal
healthcare in the United States, schools are often primary sites of access
to health education, health services, and/or diagnosis. Furthermore,
the physical, mental, and emotional health of young people, their
families, and educators are foundational to the project of education.
The connection between health and schooling was magnified during
the COVID-19 pandemic, as educators worked to not only provide
instruction but to help keep people safe and healthy. COVID-19 not
only impacted the physical, mental, and emotional well-being of students and teachers, but made it impossible to ignore the symbiotic
relationship between public health policies and policies of teaching
and learning. In this chapter, we explore how teachers made sense of,
navigated, implemented, and created policy in the midst of a world-
wide pandemic that challenged not only their work but also their
health and well-being. We focus on coalition building with families,
students, other educators, unions, and community groups as a strategy for increasing teachers' policy advocacy power.

Unsurprisingly, teachers in both Wisconsin and Massachusetts
identified multi-faceted, far-reaching impacts of COVID-19 policy
on their professional practice. Policies relating to health and safety,
remote teaching, work hour limits for teachers, and the provision of

support for basic needs, among others, all shaped teachers' daily practice, often in unintended ways. These new pandemic policies were not created or implemented in a vacuum. They were layered upon existing policies, exacerbating existing inequalities and laying bare gaps in the social safety net that long preceded the virus. Teachers responded to the barrage of new policies in real time, adjusting their practices and taking on new responsibilities even as they absorbed the impact of the pandemic on their own families and personal lives.

Teachers characterized the pandemic and its unimaginable consequences for public K–12 education as a catalyst in their relationships to educational policy. Teachers who had previously seen little relevance of high-level educational policy to their daily work were now fully attentive to any news about state and federal policy relating to schools. In addition, teachers experienced greater access to policy design around instruction, a change they attributed directly to the pandemic. Still, both novice and veteran teachers identified a gap in their capacity for policy advocacy at the district, state, or federal levels. Though Massachusetts teachers viewed the pandemic as a definite turning point in their relationship to educational policy, offering not only greater motivation but also greater opportunity to be vocal, to advocate, and to be involved in policy design, their confidence in their ability to do so were largely restricted to their own schools. Based on the data offered by teachers, we outline the strategy of coalition building as one that holds promise in responding to concerns such as those described by the teachers in this chapter.

We conceptualize coalitions as "mechanisms to bring organizations and individuals together for collective efforts ranging from short-term crisis responses to longer-term problem-solving for social change" (Greenawalt et al., 2021). Collective action between stakeholders in education works best when it is systematic and prioritized as part of teachers' professional development (Lawson et al., 2021). This chapter details teacher reflections pointing to the importance of building coalitions with a number of diverse stakeholder groups in K–12 schools including other teachers, administrators, families, community-based organizations, and advocacy organizations. Teachers' experiences also highlight the tensions and challenges in collaborative work across roles, settings, and priorities, especially as it relates to educational decision-making and policy.

We focus on coalition building in this chapter because its importance was particularly evident in the unpredictable and fast-moving conditions of COVID-19, in which educators often had to adapt on the spot with a wide range of individuals and organizations to support students and families in crisis. Activating "people power" between teachers and community stakeholders was critical not only for public health reasons and instructional purposes, but also in fighting for socially just schools as the pandemic continued to exacerbate inequities in schools and communities (McKinney de Royston & Turner, 2020). Lessons learned during the COVID-19 pandemic drive us to think about a "new normal" of family–educator engagement where decision-making and leadership is shared (Ishimaru, 2022; Mapp & Bergman, 2021). The coalition-building strategy we describe at the end of this chapter can be an important early step in this model.

IMPACT OF POLICIES ON TEACHERS

Teachers in Wisconsin and Massachusetts attempted to describe the immeasurable impact of COVID-19–related educational policies on their practice. In the earliest stages of the pandemic during the spring of 2020, Massachusetts teachers described the policy context as one of multilevel, continuous change happening on an extremely compressed timeline. One middle school teacher in Massachusetts described the unprecedented number and impact of new policies impacting teachers' work. She wrote:

> The state is setting policies for when school is open and other measures to keep ourselves and others safe. Our district has policies about what remote learning will look like. And then previously set policies and practices like technology and class size are playing into what we're doing right now. All of these different policies are determining how school is operating currently in this strange quarantine world: what we are teaching, when we are teaching it, how we are pushing materials out to the students, how much time we are spending, how much time the students should be spending, how they will access materials, how we will hold them responsible for doing the work, etc.

Student teachers, who were forming emerging understandings of what it meant to teach against the backdrop of a singular global experience, were similarly affected by the range and scope of new policies they witnessed rolling out in their schools. These new policies included those relating to mandatory class times during remote instruction, student behavior during Zoom classes, curriculum, and grading, all of which were developed and rolled out in early April of 2020.

A refrain from participants in the spring of 2020 was that teachers were working under extremely demanding conditions. To a one, the teachers in Massachusetts described the professional demands on their time and energy as untenably high, because of a steep learning curve to online instruction, new expectations born out of new policy, as well as the additional effort required simply to make sure their students were surviving. A kindergarten teacher shared the following snapshot of her work at the start of the pandemic:

> Each day, I post lessons on Seesaw for students to complete in all
> subject areas. As students complete these activities, I immediately
> correct them with comments. Some assignments I send back
> to students to fix errors. I monitor students' progress daily.
> Each night I read my students a bedtime story. We also have a
> Google Meet class each week so we can see and interact with our
> classmates. I also individually call each student's family to say
> hello, check in, and make sure they don't need anything. I write
> my students a personalized letter each week that I mail to them.

Like the teacher quoted above, all of the teachers in our groups described working more and working harder than ever before. Still, it is crucial to recognize that the different social identities held by teachers in our sample necessarily impacted the effect of the pandemic on their professional and personal lives. Although the overwhelming majority of teachers in our sample identify as White, we know that longstanding health disparities in the United States played out in COVID-19 fatalities, with Non-Hispanic Black or African American people and Hispanic people more than twice as likely to be hospitalized due to COVID-19 than non-Hispanic White people (DeSimone, 2022). The data is also clear that socioeconomic disparities impacted COVID-19 infection and hospitalization rates, indicating that teachers who were the sole wage-earners in their home faced additional challenges.

The intersection of gender and policy was a key factor in teachers' experiences with COVID-19 school policy. Teaching, like social work and nursing, is gendered as a "caring" profession, or one primarily focused on the care of other people (Noddings, 1996). Custodial care, not to mention the responsibilities of social development, have always been central to the teacher role. Though the majority of our teacher sample identified as women, some did not, and not all of the teachers in the groups had children or aging parents for whom they were responsible. Still, as one preservice teacher pointed out, many teachers were juggling multiple family and caregiving responsibilities along with their teaching responsibilities now taking place at home. This fundamental change in life circumstances necessitated a shift in availability and attention but was not always accompanied by a shift in professional expectations.

In recognition of the impact of teaching from home on teachers, districts and local unions in Massachusetts negotiated work hour restrictions. However, even policies intended to protect teachers' time had unintended consequences. Teachers agreed that work hour limits were absolutely necessary. However, they also acknowledged that boundaries around teacher work hours were not always in alignment with students' need for more assistance or teachers' personal standards for their teaching. One preservice teacher, who readily acknowledged the need for work hour limits, also recognized the unintended, unavoidable negative impact of the policy on instruction. She said:

> We are limited to three 30-minute video conferences per week per student. Which means that we have face to face time with our students for a maximum of 90 minutes each week. I wish we had more instructional time with them. In a 30-minute session, we probably spend ten minutes logging on to Zoom, and saying "Hi" and "Bye." Then if you factor in 3–4 questions from students. That's another ten minutes, which leaves about ten minutes for an activity or to teach new content.

The balance between educators' own well-being and the provision of quality instruction were sometimes positioned at odds. At the start of the COVID-19 crisis, teachers found themselves in a position of extremes. On the one hand, they were lauded as selfless heroes in popular culture. Like other essential workers, teachers were the focus of effusive public support on social media during the earliest stages of the pandemic. On the other hand, they were tasked with more unremunerated care work than ever before, both at work and at home, on top of their typical professional responsibilities. And, as the narratives in this chapter demonstrate, the positive effect of the early pandemic in public perception did not necessarily last.

As the crisis continued and teachers began to advocate for boundaries around their workload, they faced backlash from some families in their communities. One Massachusetts teacher shared, "I was on a local Facebook page and people were talking about how we [teachers] are complaining about having to work so much." A teacher in another district agreed, saying "There's a woman in our community who is actually taking pictures of teachers she knows in our town if they walk their dog for a few minutes in the middle of the day, like it's proof that we're not working hard when we're teaching at home." Teachers were bemused by the competing public perspectives on their performance as educators and essential workers.

Districts instituted other policy changes intended to ease the intense workload involved in remote instruction. One adopted by multiple districts was to have grade-level teams coconstruct shared learning plans for each week. One elementary school teacher shared, "The beginning was so hard. There were so many meetings and we changed how we were sending out the learning we were sending out every single week and trying to send out something that everyone agreed upon. It was so much trying to figure out revamping the way we taught." An elementary teacher said, "I've never collaborated so much in my life."

Teachers understood the intent of this policy to be to ensure that all students would be receiving comparable, standards-aligned instruction, as well as to create opportunities for teachers to have team support even while teaching remotely. However, the requirement to have grade-level teams develop shared learning plans for each week also increased pressure for teachers to provide the same content in lockstep. A preservice teacher explained,

> We are now teaching as a grade level. . . . The idea behind this policy is that students across the grade are all participating in the same exact activity each day to bring consistency to the student during a time of uncertainty as a community. However, I have also seen how this limits the individual teachers who like to get more creative with their curriculum. Now, it's not just that all

teachers are implementing the same curriculum, but it's that
all teachers are doing the exact same thing at the same time.

As the quote above indicates, the policy of shared learning plans
provided collaboration for teachers and consistency for students,
but also resulted in the loss of flexibility, creativity, and individual
teachers' decision-making power. All the teachers in our group had
eyes open to the benefits and drawbacks of new policies and some
of the unintended consequences that emerged over the course of the
pandemic.

Notably, preservice teachers experienced pandemic-related policy change in their teacher education programs as well as in their
field placements. Like their counterparts in the K–12 setting, states
and universities had to make decisions about how to respond to the
impact of the pandemic on faculty, staff, students, and on higher
education policy. This was certainly the case in the field of teacher
education, where existing policies had to be reexamined and new
policies had to be developed. Each of the Massachusetts preservice
teachers described how their preservice teaching experience shifted
significantly as a result of the pandemic, including but not limited to
curtailed teaching hours, moving to the online setting, and changes
in responsibilities. At various points in their training, as the pandemic dragged on, preservice teachers were uncertain about what these
changes might mean for their licensure process and their progress to
program completion. Teacher education policy was being created and
re-created in many of the same ways as K–12 education policy, and
in both contexts there was limited clarity and communication. One
preservice teacher wrote:

I do not feel that my teacher prep program or the [state
department of education] was prepared at all to support the
student teacher through this as it was so unexpected. Therefore,
I would definitely advocate for my university to become more
prepared and have plans put in place for these kinds of situations,
rather than keeping people guessing for weeks about what the
state expects from student teachers at this time.

Preservice teachers in Massachusetts saw parallel challenges between
the K–12 and higher education settings in terms of their pandemic

response. Recognizing that no teacher education program could have anticipated an event on the scale of COVID-19, preservice teachers nevertheless expressed concern about the consequences of reactive policy change on their progress to licensure and their preparation as teachers.

STUDENT WELL-BEING

All of the Massachusetts teachers desired educational policy that prioritized emotional safety and well-being for teachers, students, and families. One teacher described her primary concerns as a teacher of very young children in a diverse, socioeconomically under-resourced school community during the phase of remote-only instruction. She explained:

> [In our district we] have a lot of [English Learner] students so it's been hard to keep in contact with all the families. We have a lot of low-income families so I've delivered groceries to the families in my classroom, call to just check up, I've sent wellness checks to one student because I wasn't sure that he was in a safe situation, he's actually been removed from his house.

In the earliest weeks of the pandemic, teachers worried greatly about their students' basic needs: safety, food, housing, and health. Teachers did not always feel that educational policy developed in response to the COVID-19 crisis reflected a full awareness of the complexities of student needs during the pandemic. Teachers wanted policy to reflect the crucial role that schools play as sources of stability and constancy for communities, particularly those most vulnerable. The Massachusetts teachers felt deeply responsible for providing care, normalcy, and emotional sustenance to their students and their students' families at a time of unprecedented upheaval and fear. At the same time, teachers knew that policies clinging to a "business-as-usual" mindset could not be successful. They grappled with the tension between providing reassurance and a need for all to recognize the reality of the circumstances. One preservice teacher reflected:

> A lot of people, at least at the beginning, were thinking of school as kind of a sense of normalcy or a return to normalcy, so we

need that sense of structure, which is true, but also, we need to acknowledge that people are scared, and kids of all ages are also scared and worried about their family members who are working, or friends who are sick, and people who are making policy need to understand that school just can't be the same with all that's going on.

The powerful societal desire for school to "just be the same" was amplified as the pandemic continued. As many students in Massachusetts returned to the classroom in the 2020–2021 academic year, yet another set of new policies needed to be developed to support public safety during in-person teaching while seeking some sense of normalcy at school. Masking policy was particularly impactful for teachers' relationships with students. One middle school teacher stated, "I spend a lot of time in the hallway saying 'Pull up your mask! Put your mask on.'" A kindergarten teacher noted that for the early childhood grades, "The mask is a whole other level of behavior management added to the day. Every day after recess I have ten kids coming up to me Ms. T, Ms. T, I need a new mask! Do you have a new mask? Now I'm buying masks with my own money because the nurse is out of masks."

Social distancing policy was also impactful, particularly to teachers' pedagogical decision-making. Another kindergarten teacher described how the requirement to keep students 3 to 6 feet apart shaped her work and the experiences of the students in her classroom. She explained, "The Kindergarten kids switch classrooms for reading instruction, so they are grouped based on ability levels. With that, since the classes are intermingled, we don't sit on the rug to read a story, kids are sitting at their tables. I have them grouped based on who their teachers are. We're trying to make the best of it and try to do what we can."

In the earliest days of the pandemic, teachers faced frequently changing policies designed and implemented on a compressed timeline. As the pandemic progressed, teachers adapted to the ongoing policy churn and the shifting public perception of their newly defined responsibilities. By the later stages of the pandemic, once back at school, teachers were making sense of how to put into practice a new set of policies targeting public safety within school buildings.

COVID-19 AS CATALYST

As the narratives above illustrate, COVID-19 dramatically impacted
teachers' experiences in the classroom through the rollout of new policies. It also influenced their relationship to policy itself. Preservice
teachers, who were just learning how to teach in the spring of 2020
when the pandemic began, characterized COVID-19 policy change
as having a powerful impact on their understanding of the relevance
of educational policy in their professional lives. One preservice
teacher described how COVID-19 magnified the amount of teacher
policy work that was visible to her, explaining, "You think of state
policies or national policies, and I don't think I ever realized all
the little policies that are just at the school level or even in your
classroom. . . . Now I see how many policies you as a teacher are
involved in on a day to day basis." Another student teacher agreed,
explaining, "I think I have thought of policy before as something far
away. I knew that it affected me and that I had to follow the policies
but not that I was necessarily connected or had any sort of impact.
But what this has shown me is that policies can change quickly and
we have to change with them and that we are part of the policy."

Practicing teachers, too, identified a change in their view of the
relevance of educational policy in their daily practice, as well as an
increased awareness of the importance of federal and state policy on
their day-to-day work. Veteran teachers who had not previously believed educational policy to be particularly impactful on their every-
day practice swiftly reexamined that view. As we saw in the epigraph
to the chapter, one teacher noted a heightened relevance of state and
federal-level educational policy to day-to-day professional life:

> I've been teaching for a while now. In January it was kind of like,
> yes, I'm aware of policy, nothing really changes very quickly.
> Now I feel like I hang on to these briefings every time something
> comes on the news. I literally recorded the eleven o'clock news
> because I didn't hear all the details of the reopening plan. I feel
> like so many things about our lives and how we do our jobs are
> hanging in the balance on these minute-to-minute policies that
> are being decided. Now I feel like it has an extreme impact on
> what we're doing, how we're doing it, how we're interacting with
> our kids, the amount of time, how we prove what we're doing,
> and it has shifted my view dramatically.

The quote above illustrates a view shared by many teachers that educational policy, even at a seemingly far-away federal level, was more salient to their professional work than ever before. Notably, many teachers referenced more opportunities to make policy as a result of the pandemic. Special education teachers in Wisconsin, for example, cited an example of an "additional services policy" for students with special needs resulting from school closures in the spring of 2020. Guidance from the state Department of Public Instruction for the 2020–2021 school year suggested that students with IEPs were eligible for additional services upon the return to in-person instruction. The guidance stipulated that "the parent and school staff, or IEP team, can make decisions about 'additional services' without someone filing a state complaint or due process hearing" (Wisconsin Department of Public Instruction, 2020). In theory, individual school districts provided suggestions on how these additional services might be provided. However, in the reality of implementation, it fell to teachers to create school and classroom policy in order to operationalize the policy's stated purpose of providing more instructional time for students with IEPs. Teachers in the Wisconsin group developed interpretations of what should be considered "services" and "instruction" and shifted schedules so that students could come in before or after school to receive additional instruction. In doing so, they effectively made and implemented policy with the potential to directly shape student learning where there had been little more than suggestions provided by the state. Though teachers have always been policymakers, teachers in our groups identified increasing occasions on which directives came from states and districts with little guidance, leaving the door open for teachers to come together in their local contexts to interpret, design, and implement policy themselves.

Many Massachusetts teachers also felt that one of the unexpected outcomes of COVID-19 and its impact on schools was an increased opportunity to be involved in policy design in their school buildings. This change was accompanied by greater power and influence as well as the growing pains of new and unfamiliar ways of relating to policy. One elementary school teacher described the increased access to policy design she experienced at her school, and the resulting shift in her orientation toward her role in policy, sharing:

I have been noticing more that our principal puts a lot of policy in our hands, which at first I found frustrating, but now I am

starting to realize that it is liberating. Every other time that
another administrator or leader took policy into their own
hands with no feedback from teachers, I was very angry. . . .
We're not usually given a voice. You have to use that voice.

Preservice teachers in the Massachusetts group had a range of
views about the potential of teacher policy power brought about by
the pandemic. The degree to which preservice teachers felt optimism
around teacher involvement in policy decision-making and design
was often district- and school-dependent. One student, who was
paired with a seasoned teacher with years of experience in her school
building, described observing her supervising practitioner successfully advocate for policy change during COVID-19. She described
one experience in which school administrators disseminated a schedule at the start of virtual learning. Her teacher sent a group message questioning the rotating schedule and outlining her concerns
and suggestions. Just hours later, the administration circulated a new
schedule that incorporated her teacher's suggestions. The student
teacher stated, "I assume she was not the only one to speak up, but
even so, it gave me hope to see that a teacher raised a concern and
a change was made as a result, which reinforces the importance of
policy advocacy."

Another preservice teacher, Betsy, expressed frustration with
the difficulties of advocating for change outside of one's individual
sphere of influence. Betsy is White, in her 20s, and describes herself
as opinionated and outspoken. She spoke to the hierarchy of access
and power around the setting of policy agendas and writing of policy
texts. She wrote:

I have realized how much everyone on the teaching, planning,
and implementing level relies upon guidance from the "higher
up" on what they should be doing. Of course, they rely on this
guidance because those administrators or those superintendents
are their bosses. However, this makes me feel as if there is no
power in teachers for deciding what is right or expected, and
that the main expectation is that they follow the guidance to the
best of their ability. My thoughts about policy are now that it
does not seem as if policy makers are including all the people
that should be included in that policy development.

Betsy shared that the sheer number of new policies required by the pandemic gave her ample opportunity to see the policy process in action at her school and district. While she agreed that teacher feedback was invited and taken into consideration, she noted how few teachers in her building appeared to be involved in policy design or evaluation, a realization she found disheartening at this early stage of her career.

ADVOCACY BEYOND THE SCHOOL BUILDING

Indeed, many practicing teachers still found advocacy *beyond* their school buildings challenging in spite of increased opportunities for policy involvement and greater experience with policy advocacy as a result of the pandemic. For example, one Massachusetts teacher stated, "I definitely don't know how to make change in the bigger [context]. I guess I go to the grade level leader, and then the grade level leader goes to the principal, and then the principal goes to the superintendent."

The policy problem of returning to in-person instruction in the fall of 2020 offers insight into teachers' lack of self-efficacy around policy advocacy beyond their school buildings. Although the transition to in-person teaching was of critical importance to them, the Massachusetts teachers were cautious about advocating in favor of any particular policy approach. Teachers were certain that they did not feel comfortable advocating around whether and when to reopen school buildings. As one teacher stated, "We're not public health officials." Another explained further, "I wouldn't want to be part of some decisions because I'm not an expert, but I would want to be involved in the question of *how* we go back [to school in the fall]." Of course, not all teachers experienced this topic in the same way. Teachers in lower-resourced districts had to contend with basic challenges to safety, including, for example, poorly ventilated classrooms or insufficient space to physically distance. The nature of exactly what condition teachers across the country would be returning to when schools reopened necessarily impacted attitudes toward COVID-19 back-to-school debates.

Some teachers were willing to trust in the decision-making of school, district, state, and federal administrators, citing the positive intent they identified in other policy-level decisions made during the pandemic. One preservice teacher reflected, "I find that the policies being established right now are done with everyone's best effort. It's not like in the past, when I would have thought, 'Why are we doing this?' Every teacher and administrator I talk with is giving 110% of themselves to these policies." However, other teachers wanted greater capacity for advocacy beyond their grade-level teams and school buildings, highlighting what they viewed as a distinct moment and opportunity for teacher voice in policy. A teacher argued:

> If we're not going to say anything right now, when is our chance? When are we going to ask for help or stand up or push back or say that's not right or that's not developmentally appropriate? Teachers are flocking out of teaching right now. There's not enough support saying what can we do to keep you here? How are you? How can we support you? If we don't speak up, there's going to be a mass exodus.

These sentiments were echoed by a preservice teacher in Wisconsin, who offered the following thoughts relating to the need for a collective recognition of the intense changes that have taken place in education as a result of the pandemic:

> I think that there needs to be a school-wide or district-wide meeting discussing what is working, what is not, and what we can change going into the future—reflecting on how COVID-19 and two years at home virtual learning impacted students and what we can do to accommodate their needs moving forward. It is not the best solution to just continue with business as usual because COVID-19 has really impacted schools and educators all across the nation and it is a totally new experience for everyone.

Other preservice teachers talked about their desire for more advocacy power in the higher education setting, referencing COVID-related policy changes impacting preservice teachers as teacher candidates. None of the preservice teachers in our Massachusetts group felt they had a say in those changes. One wrote, "I would like to know why none of the student teachers were included in these conversations, but rather sent vague emails about the guidance that the state is sending to our program." The preservice teacher wondered at what point, if any, in the policy process, preservice teachers who were the foci of teacher preparation policy might have an opportunity to weigh in on decisions impacting their professional training, licensure, and future careers.

HIGH-LEVERAGE STRATEGY: COALITION BUILDING

In this section, we highlight coalition building as a strategy for increasing teachers' engagement with and impact on policy by fostering sustained connections between teachers and members of other potential partner groups. We conceptualize coalitions as "mechanisms to bring organizations and individuals together for collective efforts ranging from short-term crisis responses to longer-term problem-solving for social change" (Greenawalt et al., 2021). In the data presented throughout this chapter, teachers' experiences showcase policy problems around which coalitions can be of support, including but not limited to supporting teacher policy advocacy around immediate and acute responses to a crisis (such as the policy demands brought on by COVID-19) as well as bigger-picture systemic change (such as the capacity and agency of teachers for policy advocacy as a whole).

Teachers in Massachusetts and Wisconsin described how their work intersected with that of a range of other groups as they negotiated COVID-19 pressures. These groups included other teachers, families and parent organizations, community-based organizations, institutions of higher education, policy advocacy organizations, and other professionals serving students and families. Below, we detail the possibilities for coalitions that emerged from our data, describing the affordances and challenges of each and offering suggestions for how individuals in a range of policy positions can encourage connections across silos.

With Teachers

Teachers in both states emphasized the importance of connections with other teachers, whether in a hallway conversation, a professional conference, or across the country via social media. Teachers in Wisconsin, for example, talked about ways to avoid being on "educator island." One teacher described wanting networks that could be sustained beyond a single issue or encounter. They stated:

We need to make sure we are not isolated. That there are people
we trust when we face the challenges we do during the day.
Be connected in a way that is useful for you. Being connected
shouldn't be more work. That is something powerful that came
out of [recent statewide policy], that banding together. Yes, we
can go out and protest, but we also can email about challenges
they face. It extends past the first reason we came together.

As the quote above indicates, teachers wanted ways of building
networks that were nimble and accessible. They talked about different spaces and platforms that facilitate connections with others, both
in real life and in digital spaces. Before COVID-19, in-person conferences and legislative or lobbying events provided important spaces for
teachers to connect. Many of these went virtual or hybrid in 2020,
2021, and 2022 because of public health concerns, but nonetheless
facilitated network building with teachers.

Social media has been a critically important space for teachers to connect around policy activism and advocacy efforts (Niesz
& D'Amato, 2021; Seelig et al., 2019) that has flourished given the
constraints on in-person gatherings. Connections made possible by
social media outlets can encourage greater participation in advocacy
and inspire more interaction between teachers. Teachers can consider professional engagement in media spaces, such as a Facebook
group of special education teachers, or might engage in policy advocacy around a particular issue they learn about on social media, such
as a post on Twitter announcing a rally at a state capitol on special
education policy changes. These platforms provide ways for teachers
to connect with peers and build coalitions that do not require geographic proximity, travel time, or sidelining of other professional or
personal responsibilities.

Collaboration with teachers' unions was another key theme in
teachers' policy engagement during the pandemic. Not all teachers
came into the pandemic period as strong supporters of their union,
particularly if they were reluctant to be viewed as challenging administrative authority. Some teachers believed that union involvement
might be negatively interpreted by their school building leaders. Union
representatives played an important role in assuaging teachers' fears
about union participation, particularly for those without the protection of tenure. A novice teacher reported, "Our representative who
manages the union is also a teacher at my school. And at the meetings,

she'll shut the door. She'll shut the windows. 'Nothing you say is going to leave this space. I am also a teacher here and I represent you.' And then she follows up. I've seen that first-hand."

Teachers described the union as a central player in negotiating policy, advocating for members' needs, and giving member teachers access to amplified policy voice during the public health crisis. A Massachusetts teacher explained:

> The union was super powerful. We haven't had a lot of need for
> that in the past besides the years that we're negotiating a contract.
> That is one place where things really came up because of COVID.
> The amount of time I spent in union meetings and ratifying this
> or that Memorandum of Understanding! It was really contentious
> with the district which has not been our history with the district
> or the school committee. That's a place where advocacy was
> a huge thing because of all of the things that needed to be
> negotiated and all of the policies; trying to keep the teachers safe,
> trying to keep the students safe, what's the best way to have time
> on learning, user technology, all these different things.

After witnessing their local unions' work during COVID-19, multiple Massachusetts teachers described a new view of participation in the union as itself a form of policy advocacy. A preservice teacher stated, "I do see being in the local union as being a local change-maker." As the pandemic continued, even teachers who had previously been skeptical about their union were convinced of their union's importance. Previously, some teachers had had limited confidence in the union's utility or had had fears about how union membership would be perceived by administrators. Unions' roles as supportive, protective units, as well as their tangible successes negotiating for better working conditions for teachers in many districts, were brought to the fore during the crisis. Bolstering relationships between union leadership and members can lead to greater trust and confidence, and stronger coalitions across teachers.

With Administrators

The teachers who described being active in union membership in the section above acknowledged that union participation could be viewed as a challenge to the administration.

However, teachers also explained that positive relationships with building leaders could not only mitigate those tensions, but support mutually respectful, collegial, and positive relationships with administration. They described positive relationships between teachers and administrators as requiring time, trust, and investment on the part of both sides, but ultimately beneficial for all, including students. A middle school teacher explained,

> I would certainly advocate for building strong relationships with your admin team. It's really necessary. It really is. I am so pleased with our admin team and that makes it easy for me to speak up, get involved, share my two cents. Because I know that they value me as an educator, and they think I have something to offer. They've shown me that. I would tell a novice teacher to do that. To make those relationships.

Like the teacher quoted above, many teachers in the Massachusetts group framed relationship building with administrators to be a matter of individual choice. They recognized, of course, inherent differences between the roles and experiences of administrators and classroom teachers, but nevertheless believed that teachers could, if desired, opt to develop relationships of respect, trust, and appreciation with administrators that could lead to the identification of shared goals. At the same time, teachers encouraged administrators to take the initiative to create pathways for teacher participation in school policy design, to foster a climate of collaboration, and to explicitly invite all teachers to the discussion in ways that make evident their commitment to distributed policy leadership.

With Families

Teachers described collaboration with parents and families as critical to their success in the classroom, citing multiple ways teachers and families could work together to support students both academically and in a way that honors their social–emotional health. Informal, one-on-one partnerships between teachers and families are indispensable to the flourishing of students. However, when it came to educational policy, teachers in Massachusetts often characterized the relationship between teachers and parents and guardians to be at odds. In describing the influence of parents over policy in her district, one teacher stated, "The parents *are* the policymakers." Indeed, many of the Massachusetts teachers viewed parents and families as having greater policy capacity and agency than teachers, based on their experience with teachers voicing concerns and dissatisfactions around curriculum, class assignments, scheduling, and other topics.

At the beginning of the pandemic, teachers in Massachusetts reported overwhelming support from families in their communities. As the pandemic stretched on and debates around whether, when, and how to go back to in-person instruction arose, however, teachers often found themselves on opposite sides of the table from parents and guardians. In one focus group, a preservice teacher who was a parent in a different district than the one in which she was student teaching described receiving a letter regarding the conditions for fall reopening under COVID. She and another practicing teacher had the following exchange:

> *Preservice teacher/Parent:* They sent home an email this week asking parents to vote. I'm a parent, and they said, "We won't make a decision until every parent has logged in to vote."
>
> *Practicing teacher:* I'm dying to know if they asked the teachers. I love how they're not going to change until parents respond. I'd love to know if every teacher had to respond.
>
> *Preservice teacher/Parent:* I guess I'm part of the policymakers here in my town at least. When I responded back to the principal, I cc-d my son's teacher just for her to be aware of what's going on.

The theme of the family role in educational settings was an important one in teachers' discussions of policy before and during the pandemic. As noted in previous chapters, COVID-19 impacted parents' involvement in educational decision-making in a number of ways. Wisconsin teachers at an EdCamp reflected on how parents and guardians were closer to the classroom than ever before, seeing, hearing, and participating in it on their students' Chromebooks while sitting next to them at the kitchen table. Teachers discussed the unintended consequences of school taking place in homes during remote learning. Although they viewed it as positive when families are more aware of their children's learning, teachers were concerned about parents and guardians wanting to more closely review and comment on curriculum. One teacher described parents as "considerably louder" in the 2021–2022 academic year about what they viewed as "acceptable" in curriculum and instruction, a change they attributed at least in part to increased parental familiarity with online instruction. They noted that this sense of familiarity was still just a partial window into the classroom, sometimes giving a misleading view of teachers' work. Teachers argued parents and caregivers believed that what they observed during remote instruction, only part of the work of teaching, comprised the full scope and complexity of what teachers were doing every day during the pandemic.

Teachers' mixed experiences with families around educational decision-making demonstrate the importance of two key factors: open communication and the identification of shared common goals and interests. There must be purposeful spaces for teachers and parents to speak openly about the school experience from their own unique vantage points. Coming together in respectful and intentional discussion sets the stage for the identification of common goals and interests. When teachers and families are able to craft collaborative agendas based on shared priorities, as we have seen happen around standardized testing, for example, they have the potential to build a formidably impactful coalition.

With Advocacy Groups

Advocacy groups and teachers also have potential for coalition building. Though Massachusetts teachers expressed interest in involvement with nonprofits and organizations relating to teacher policy advocacy, they identified a number of challenges in doing so. The first challenge identified by teachers was that involvement with advocacy groups would require time away from the classroom. A teacher stated, "Many times when you advocate for students [beyond the school building] you are pulled away from your classroom and have to supply sub lesson plans and are constantly worrying about how the day is going. That added stress does not make it enticing to want to advocate and leave the classroom for the day."

Second, teachers cited a lack of information about the advocacy groups, their scope, and how to get in contact with them. One teacher who was involved with a number of teacher professional groups on-line identified some supportive possibilities, explaining:

> Having a stipend for teachers to advocate for their students and districts would be an incentive. Having advocacy groups reach out to teachers who are in the field for advice would be helpful. Knowing what support groups are out there for teachers to contact to be advocates would be helpful. As a teacher I don't know the correct agencies to contact to become more involved to advocate for my students.

The teacher quoted above raised multiple areas for attention, including broader networks of support, financial compensation for teachers' involvement in partnership with advocacy groups, and op-portunities for advocacy groups to do more outreach. Social media platforms do provide opportunities for members of advocacy groups to connect with teachers. Twitter, Facebook, and other social media sites allow for efficient dissemination of information about events, critical knowledge related to educational policies and advocacy ef-forts, and publicity about the nature of advocacy work taking place in the nonprofit sector. Advocacy groups can leverage social media avenues to better effect in seeking to activate teachers' awareness of their groups' work and to engage teachers in ways that do not require time away from teaching.

CONCLUSION

Several important themes emerge in examining how COVID-related policies impacted teachers' experience and relationship to policy. First, teachers were unanimous in their assessment of the far-reaching and sometimes unintended impacts of the pandemic on their work as teachers, their relationships with students, and existing educational inequalities. Their experiences illustrate how the pandemic has under-scored the stark disparities in our societal structures, such as the lack of adequate social and material support for families living in poverty and families raising students with disabilities. They reflected on how COVID-19 has forced ongoing cycles of "pandemic teaching." As one practicing teacher in Wisconsin reflected, "I can't ever imagine we will be out of crisis mode, we will only be in a space where we can sustain in a crisis."

Second, the intersection of gender, power, and policy impacted the profession and the individuals within it. Women, to whom the labor of child care often falls, had multilayered responsibilities of taking care of students at school while also caring for children and parents in their own homes. Not surprisingly, women have left the workforce at higher rates during COVID, in large part as a result of the burden of these multiple shifts (Fry, 2022).

Third, teachers viewed the tremendous uncertainty and risk in education at this time as increasing their awareness of the importance of educational policy in the teaching profession. Teachers who had previously had limited interest in district, state, or federal educational policy described themselves as increasingly attentive to policy discussions at all levels. Teachers also identified the need for new policy during the pandemic as having created conditions for greater teacher involvement in policy design. At the same time, they called for greater training and resources for advocacy beyond their grade levels and school buildings, in part due to their increased awareness of the significance of policy at multiple levels of influence. As local policy became even more important than usual and had to interact with other types of policy, teachers in Massachusetts and Wisconsin wished to be better equipped to seize the opportunity for more inclusive and impactful policy involvement.

The data in this chapter points to the necessity of coalition building with others invested in specific policy areas as a means of increasing knowledge, resources, and power around policy advocacy. The case of COVID-19 educational policy is a rich background against which to examine this strategy because of its scale, impact, and urgency. However, teachers' narratives also support the utility of coalitions relating to different policy issues including but not limited to public health. For example, one Wisconsin teacher identified the potential for coalition power in reducing food waste in schools, stating, "I think it would be most helpful to have large groups of students, families, and educators who are willing to talk about how to 'fight' for these outcomes. Teachers, school staff, and administration gathering as much food waste data as possible would be most helpful." We argue that the types of coalitions described in this chapter, whether with administrators and teachers within a school building, with teachers' unions in a district, or with organizations and teacher educators at the state level or beyond, are critical to the success of teacher advocacy in a wide range of policy areas.

DISCUSSION QUESTIONS

1. In this chapter, the narratives point to the ways that teachers' social identities impacted how they experienced the COVID-19 public health crisis. What are ways that various social identities impact how policymakers in your context think about and engage with policy?
2. In many cases, teachers' policy interests align with those of other groups. How can leaders of advocacy groups, for example, be more effective in building coalitions with teachers in ways that can move educational policy in mutually beneficial ways? What happens when policy interests aren't aligned?
3. In this chapter, teachers referenced their experiences with public support and critique of teachers' work in their communities. How does public perception of teachers and their work shape educational policy? How might formal coalitions between teachers and parents, for example, emphasize policy interests shared by both groups?

CHAPTER 4

Digital Learning Policy

> We've found tools that are really helpful and I'm still using way more
> technology than I used to. I have to think about how much screen time
> these kids are doing but it saves time. Before the pandemic I spent so
> much time standing at a copy machine, sending something to the printer,
> I saw what a time saver it was to push stuff out online. I'm still re-
> navigating how we do things now that we know that we can do it online.
>
> —Practicing teacher, Massachusetts

In step with the vast array of electronic devices that have entered
the market over the last few decades, K–12 schools have seen a dramatic increase in the use of digital tools for instructional purposes
(Delgado et al., 2015; Heinrich et al., 2020). Curriculum has moved
away from textbook-centered instruction to hybrid, fully-online,
and video formats. Assessments of all kinds are housed on digital
platforms. Instruction itself now occurs both in-person and online,
in both synchronous and asynchronous modalities. Teachers increasingly communicate with students, families, and one another using a
wide variety of digital formats. The integration of digital tools has
had a broad impact on teaching practice and has changed how we
conceive of the role of the teacher and their expertise.

As a result of these shifts, schools and districts have invested heavily in hardware, software, Internet access, and staff capacity needed to
facilitate online learning. In addition, decision-makers at the state,
district, and local levels have had to design an array of policies to address digital tools and their use, including policies such as the federal
subsidizing of digital learning and the allocation of Title I funds, and
district subsidies for the purchase of student devices.

The abrupt closing of schools in the spring of 2020 led to a seis-
mic shift in how we think about digital tool policies, high-quality
instruction, and educational equity. This chapter begins with a brief

discussion of teachers' reflections on digital learning from before 2020, but it focuses primarily on teacher experiences navigating the tremendous impact of the COVID-19 pandemic on digital learning policy. We draw from data collected from preservice and practicing teachers in Massachusetts during the early stages of the COVID-19 pandemic into the 2021–2022 school year; reflections from practicing teachers from Wisconsin EdCamp sessions both before COVID-19 and during the 2021–2022 school year; and from preservice teacher workshops in the winter of 2022. We explore how teachers in Wisconsin and Massachusetts make sense of, implement, and advocate around school, district, and state policies relating to digital tools in schools. Finally, we propose the strategy of visual mapping as one with promise in responding to teachers' needs for greater advocacy power relating to digital learning policy.

Teachers in both states described their experiences with policies relating to 1:1 digital device initiatives, varying degrees of access to high-quality Internet, and unequal resource allocation, with a particular emphasis on the time of remote instruction during the pandemic. They pointed to the policy context preceding the public health crisis as setting the stage for districts' success or difficulty in pivoting to online instruction. Teachers described how during the height of the pandemic they became adept at adapting and sometimes creating digital policy on the fly, developing classroom-level policies related to digital tool use in response to the chaotic and fluid context of COVID. They also described their sensemaking around how to approach digital tool use in their classrooms late in the pandemic, given the significant freedom afforded them in local policy. Though policy implementation was part of their professional work long before COVID, teachers reported making and remaking policy more than ever before. Informed by the findings presented in this chapter, we recommend the mapping strategy as one that shows promise in providing teachers with the kind of tangible, actionable, collaborative professional development that can support growth in policy advocacy skills relating to digital policy use and beyond.

Mapping is a strategy where teachers create visual representations of how concepts, networks, people, organizations, and power connect related to policy issues that matter to them. Sometimes known as diagramming, mapping is an established way to help learners of all ages organize knowledge and concepts to better see connections (Schroeder et al., 2017). In addition to concretizing knowledge, skills, and concepts of policy and advocacy, the process of designing maps prompts deep discussion about implicit assumptions and unexamined beliefs. Mapping promotes critical thinking among learners, prompting them to dig deeper with "why," "how," "who" questions (Zandvakill et al., 2019). Importantly, mapping supports teachers in moving from conceptualization to the identification of attainable action steps relating to policy and advocacy.

Two different types of maps, "concept maps" and "power network maps," are used in our workshops to build teachers' understanding of policy advocacy and to facilitate their actionable plans. In both Massachusetts and Wisconsin, we invited teacher participants to engage in mapping exercises at the start of our work together and returned to these maps as a process tool as well as a guide for future action. We go into greater detail in subsequent sections in this chapter on how mapping can be an effective strategy for prompting teachers to engage in policy dialogue and action.

TEACHERS AND DIGITAL LEARNING POLICY BEFORE COVID-19

Even before the COVID-19 pandemic, teachers had clear opinions about how to strengthen digital learning policies in their respective schools and districts. One EdCamp session from 2017 illustrates the depth and nuance with which teachers dissected policy relating to digital learning as it existed in their local context. In this case, a group of Wisconsin teachers reflected on a recent statewide policy proposal to fund a 1:1 device initiative (i.e., a device for every student) for all high school students in the state. Participants in the session were from a variety of districts and had varied experience with 1:1 initiatives, with some districts having fully implemented programs and others at the early stages of piloting with one school. Much of the discussion revolved around whether and how districts could effectively operationalize a 1:1 device initiative given the demands of staff training, the logistics in managing devices, and potential challenges of family buy-in. Teachers in the session also discussed the layers of policy rollout: how proposed state policy for high school students could require district policy selecting which schools and grades would pilot the policy, which would then demand school policy around rules for device use at school and at home, as well as classroom policy relating to instructional use and logistics.

Three central themes emerged from the Wisconsin teachers' analysis of 1:1 device policy pre-COVID. First, in defining the policy issue, teachers interrogated the motivations for district 1:1 initiatives and how district policies defined the policy problem. Teachers identified one possible motivation as the growing range of students' varied academic needs and the affordances of digital tools for differentiated instruction. Teachers viewed universal 1:1 initiatives as potentially offering more equitable access to digital devices for students at home and staff in the classroom. Further, teachers believed that 1:1 device initiatives could broaden and diversify the information and perspectives brought into learning spaces, potentially facilitating more inclusive and culturally responsive classrooms.

Second, Wisconsin teachers emphasized the critical importance of implementation in the ultimate efficacy of 1:1 device initiatives. They had specific recommendations for how implementation in the proposed state policy could better support its success. For example, one teacher suggested creating a staged process of cohorts for 1:1 device rollout in which a first year of planning would be followed by a second year of implementation heavily supported by the district and a third year of implementation with monitoring and assessment of the policy initiative. Another teacher stated, "Support, support, support. . . . Keep the conversation constant and at the forefront."

The third overarching theme in teachers' discussions related to how digital tool policies would necessarily impact other school policies. As one teacher stated, schools adopting 1:1 digital device initiatives must "actually have staff devoted to this, because if you don't then it falls on other people (i.e., librarians) to do the repair, support. Teachers won't take risks if they don't have any support." Another teacher argued there would also need to be a policy to support time during the school day to work with other teachers and collaborate, saying "The tech skills will come when you have time to work with each other." A third teacher pointed out that policies around student use of devices would need to be implemented. In his view, if there were to be a school policy that Chromebooks were not to go home with students, then there also would need to be a policy that online homework could not be assigned, since not all students could be presumed to have access to devices at home. Teachers in the pre-COVID-19 Wisconsin EdCamp session offered the following guiding questions for legislators on the proposed statewide 1:1 device initiative, based on their own expertise and experiences:

1. What would happen to districts already doing 1:1 initiatives? For example, would there be flexibility for districts who already have devices to use the money to support staff instead of buying new devices?
2. Would there be flexibility to purchase specific devices that best fit the needs and capacity of the school and district?
3. What support would there be for teacher training, both for how to teach online but also for how to use the specific devices purchased?

The example of the Wisconsin EdCamp demonstrates the depth and nuance with which teachers made sense of and analyzed digital device policy long before the intense digital tool use of the pandemic. Teachers thought carefully about the premise upon which digital device policies in their districts and schools were built, learned from the glitches in implementation they witnessed, and developed concrete ways to improve future policy. Less clear, however, was the degree to which teachers felt that their recommendations had an avenue or an audience, whether within their buildings with principals and other administrators, or with legislators or other decisionmakers.

DIGITAL LEARNING POLICY DURING COVID-19

Teachers' experiences with digital tool policy expanded dramatically with the abrupt start of remote instruction in the spring of 2020. In the section that follows, we share reflections from teachers in both states as they contended with the rapidly changing landscape of digital learning at that time. We focus primarily on the experiences of those in Massachusetts. We describe themes and patterns chronologically, as the constantly changing circumstances of schooling in the pandemic presented critically important context to what digital learning policy looked like and how teachers engaged with it.

Digital Learning Policy in 2020

Immediately after schools closed in March 2020, digital tool use became the pressing topic in the experiences of the Massachusetts teachers in our group. Teachers who had previously had relatively little experience with digital tools were suddenly required to use them exclusively. Preservice teachers trained to develop and implement lesson plans face-to-face were forced to learn an entirely new approach to teaching in a compressed time frame. One preservice teacher stated in late April of 2020, "I am still learning to be a teacher in the classroom–I now have to learn to be a teacher remotely." Faced with no alternative but to climb the learning curve as quickly as possible, teachers in this group reported significantly increasing their capacity relating to specific digital platforms and online instructional delivery as a whole. A preservice teacher reflected, "I feel like the silver lining is that my technology skills have come a long way. I've learned a lot of different apps that you can use in education. I've gotten experience in teaching on Zoom, muting and unmuting, sharing my screen, and being the host of my Zoom classroom."

A recurring theme across practicing and preservice teachers in the Massachusetts group was the heavy workload accompanying the exclusive use of digital tools, even after the initial shock of adjustment. Though the numerous platforms and programs were often marketed as easing the pedagogical burden on teachers, the variety of tools at teachers' disposal did not alleviate their workload. In fact, the adoption of more digital tools was accompanied by an increase in expectations for teacher work. One middle school teacher described the impact of digital tool use on the quantity and frequency of student assignments expected by her administration and the ensuing demand for teacher assessment. She stated, "I feel like I'm working way harder than I did in person. I would never normally in my middle school Spanish class give three to five things that I needed to grade in a week for my 126 kids and have them back before the next week's stuff." The teacher described not only a significant increase in her workload, but a shift in her pedagogical approach to instruction and assessment in her classes.

A kindergarten teacher with many years of teaching experience described the zero-to-sixty transition from limited digital tool use to multiple digital platforms in her classroom and the demanding workload that accompanied the transition to full-time digital learning. She wrote:

> Grades K, 1, and 2 were told their online learning platform would be SeeSaw, Lexia, and DreamBox. We also signed our classes up for Happy Numbers, Epic, Storyline Online, Let's Find Out, Mystery Science, Boom Cards, etc. Each day I post

lessons on SeeSaw for students to complete in all subject areas. I monitor students' progress daily on Lexia, DreamBox, and Happy Numbers.

This teacher's use of multiple digital tools was not unique to her experience. Some of the tools listed by teachers preceded the pandemic and were already in use in schools and classrooms. Others, however, were adopted to approximate face-to-face instruction as part of districts' pandemic response. Teachers welcomed any means of connecting with their students and engaging their interest, especially at the start of virtual learning. At the same time, they named the substantial resources of time and effort necessary for teachers to become familiar with each new tool, not to mention the work involved in teaching students to use them. They were also keenly aware of family and caregivers' expectations for written comments on student work completed at home in the absence of face-to-face feedback.

Universally, teachers in the group reported having little, if any, awareness of the decision-making leading to the selection of tools or the companies with whom districts entered into agreement. None of the Massachusetts teachers were asked for input about which programs to acquire or how to implement their rollout. They noted, however, the significant financial investment that such agreements must have represented.

Furthermore, not all teachers experienced digital learning policy in the same way. Some districts had pre-existing policies that afforded greater capacity for digital tool policy rollout, such as the 1:1 digital policies described in the previous section. Pre-COVID-19 1:1 policies had been developed to address issues such as the need for greater individualization, access to supplemental instruction without additional staffing, and developing "21st Century" skills. A teacher from a middle-class suburban district described how her district's policy context prior to COVID-19 eased the transition to remote learning. She explained, "Our students are already 1-to-1 [with devices] in the middle and high school, and as a result we are farther ahead than many districts with our technology know-how and availability. The technology goals and policies have unknowingly set us up very well for this unexpected transition to remote learning." Similarly, a high school teacher in a different suburban district explained how existing policies and resources in her district eased some aspects of the transition to remote learning. She explained, "Our district was implementing ALD days, Alternative Learning Days, since last year. [That means that] in lieu of snow days we would do work-from-home days, so we were already kind of familiar with it and our students were familiar with it. . . . Our district was kind of up and running with the whole ALD format." As these teachers suggest, the level of resources available in their suburban districts impacted both the level of readiness and ability to adapt quickly. This often was not the case in under-resourced districts.

Teachers in other districts scrambled to implement digital tool-based instruction in response to COVID. Unlike those who had had the foresight and the resources to implement 1:1 device initiatives without the catalyst of a global pandemic, many districts had to craft policy as a response to a very different problem: basic access to instruction. Districts that had not previously had the option of offering Chromebooks to each of their students now had state and federal support to do so, and needed to roll out this new policy quickly and under challenging conditions. In some cases, devices waited in boxes in school hallways as administrators worked furiously to distribute them. Staffing of bus drivers, concerns about efficient, safe hand-off, and varying levels of comfort with technology among families were all challenging factors. Even once plans were in place, there was no certainty that distribution would result in successful device use. In the early stage of the pandemic, one teacher in a district with a large percentage of students living in poverty explained, "Students within my class . . . do not have access to a device for a variety of reasons, including not coming to school to pick up the device, not having Internet, having a device but not allowing students to use the device, having the device but not understanding what to do with it."

One of the challenges described by teachers was that of reliable Internet access. Though many districts negotiated Internet access for previously unserved families through local Internet providers, the roll-out of these initiatives was thorny. Faced with the lag in implementation, a kindergarten teacher in an economically diverse district wrote, "I have been advocating for a second paper and pencil packet to be sent home to families who will not use devices, who do not have Internet, or have not completed any work up to this point." Ultimately, without confirmation of Internet availability in students' homes, districts, schools, and teachers could not ensure access to instruction. As a result, teachers had to consider the fundamental challenge of inequality of access in planning their daily instruction. As a preservice teacher wrote, "In order to reach all students, each remote activity that is rolled out must consider these factors: do any students still need a device with internet? Do they have internet access at home?" Teachers reported developing assignments that could be disseminated electronically as well as in hard copy, in some cases driving to students' homes to drop off paper versions of assignments. Problems of inequitable access and resources at the state, district and school levels that have always existed in relation to digital tool policy were greatly amplified in the context of the pandemic.

Inequity manifested itself in other ways that were impactful on student learning. Parents and guardians who were essential workers and unable to sit with their children to monitor schoolwork during the day were forced to choose between having their children stay up late to complete their work or having them not complete it at all. One teacher stated, "I have very young students submitting their work with timestamps that say midnight, 1 o'clock. But their parents work, and they want to support their children. What can I say?" When the use of digital tools for the completion of schoolwork requires the guidance of an adult, students who need assistance have to wait for a caregiver to be available. Households in which adults work long hours or second and third shifts yet remain committed to supporting their children's learning see no viable option but to adjust students' schedules accordingly.

Virtual learning, challenging under the best of circumstances, brought with it additional complications for teachers of some groups of students. For example, districts in Massachusetts with high percentages of English learners not only struggled with delivery of quality instruction, but also with effective communication with families relating to digital device use and the myriad of new software programs being rolled out. Instructions on how to use tools and programs needed to be communicated in multiple languages and made accessible in different modalities. Students, families, and teachers in special education settings also faced increased challenges. First, providing access to digital devices appropriate to student needs with the full instructional appropriateness of the online learning environment in mind (Hurwitz et al., 2021; Sayman & Cornell, 2021) was of special impact for students receiving special education services. Second, for students entitled to one-to-one aides in the school context, virtual learning at home without additional teacher support in the earliest days of the pandemic was incredibly difficult.

By the end of the spring semester of 2020, most schools across the country were still holding classes fully online. Teachers did their utmost to provide equal access to high-quality, engaging instruction remotely while navigating digital learning policies that vastly increased their workload. This included taking IEPs, language factors, and the availability of family support into account as they planned and delivered instruction. Above all, teachers continued to worry about the students they were not able to serve.

Digital Learning Policy in 2021-2022

By the fall of 2021, as the new academic year began, the teachers in the Massachusetts cohort had wide-ranging views on the history and future of digital tool use in the classroom. As a group, they looked back on digital tool use during earlier phases of the pandemic as necessary to keep school going. Later, once schools were largely back to face-to-face instruction, however, teachers had mixed feelings about whether that sacrifice was still warranted. Districts continued to use disparate approaches to digital tool use and, given that few had official policies mandating a specific number of platforms or the frequency of their use, teachers had free rein to set their own expectations. Some teachers made the intentional choice to move away from the heavy reliance on digital tools, especially at the younger grade levels. A kindergarten teacher in a suburban district explained:

> This year, the feeling is that digital learning is awesome, but our students are so young. We're not really using any technology this year because after spending the last year or two staring at a screen, that's the last thing any of us wanted this year. At my grade level, in my school, we don't have any requirements to use any digital learning platforms, so our choice was not to use those. It almost flipped backwards.

Teachers in districts or schools that did have official guidance around digital learning sometimes found the policies constraining. One elementary school teacher described a tension between her personal philosophy and her school policy, saying, "There's this huge focus on—we want students to have 60 minutes on Lexia every week. This may just be me, but after the pandemic I want them to get off screens as much as I can. I want them outside as much as I can. I want them moving their bodies." This teacher referenced research on the impact of screen time on children's developing brains, noting the irony of sending children to school in person only to have them learn via an online tool. She connected the push for more reading time on the digital tool with broader assessment and accountability pressures, explaining:

> I get so frustrated when people say our numbers are so
> low, if we use these apps on their Chromebooks for targeted
> instruction, it will target their weaknesses. Sixty minutes a week
> they want me to use a math intervention app, another sixty
> minutes a week they're using Lexia. What if they're having an
> amazing conversation about a book they just read? I'm supposed
> to say stop, everyone put on their headphones and go on Lexia?
> I feel pressure to do all these district initiatives so that they can
> track the data. I understand that you want to track growth,
> but what is the meaning of education? Why are we here?

The teacher quoted above raised the question of the relationship between digital tool policy and assessment policy. The progression of digital platforms and software under COVID-19 led to districts and schools moving toward using information gathered from student use of digital tools as data. Students' scores on online math games, their logged reading minutes on Lexia, and the number of correct answers in word work programs all had potential as a set of data for measuring learning. Teachers were accustomed to the need to gather markers of student learning, but worried about digital learning usurping other critically important elements of inquiry.

Other teachers were more enthusiastic about the benefits of carrying over specific aspects of online instruction to their in-person teaching. For example, teachers identified individual digital tools that they viewed as additive to their teaching. One Massachusetts teacher described using slides created for remote learning, as well as using Lexia, DreamBox, and Raz-Kids, programs for which her district had purchased subscriptions during the pandemic. Because COVID-19 regulations made it challenging for her to work with students in small groups after the return to in-person instruction, she leveraged the digital tools as a means of differentiation.

In another example, Wisconsin teachers at an EdCamp in February 2022 reflected on the benefits of parents and guardians having greater access to the "classroom" during virtual learning, in which family members had unprecedented access to observe the goings-on of the class. They recognized the affordances of digital tool use for parents and guardians to participate in conferences and meetings given varying work and life schedules. Both practicing and preservice special education teachers in Wisconsin noted, for example, the increase in accessibility to IEP meetings because of new virtual options.

At the same time, many teachers identified unintended negative consequences of student access to digital tools at home. Digital devices are often touted as supporting equity by leveling the field of who has access to a computer at home, though, as described earlier, the experiences of rolling out device distribution and Internet service involved multiple challenges for districts in this study. However, teachers also distinguished between having a device at home and using that device at home for the purposes of instructional advancement, pointing to new problems of digital tool policy in the later pandemic period. For example, continuous access to devices in the classroom was often accompanied by classroom management problems. In a Wisconsin preservice teacher discussion in Spring 2022, teachers identified a key implementation issue relating to "inconsistencies in expectations and enforcement surrounding device use and game play." Teachers saw potential for teacher advocacy relating to clear, consistent, teacher-led policy relating to inappropriate use of digital tools. Asked to develop a pitch statement for a possible solution to the policy problem, teachers developed the following:

> I propose we decide, as a staff, what our expectations for non-academic technology (video games, videos not related to school) use should be. Once this has been decided on, we will present the expectations to students, and enforce them consistently.
> I hope to minimize ambiguity in our enforcement of technology expectations, and that we are fair in holding students to the same standards.

That the teachers above suggested an approach of shared decision-making and uniform application of the rules indicates that, at least in their districts, these practices were not in place. Other teachers indicated that there was also a need for training in the use of specific digital tools and their relationship to high-quality, effective pedagogy. One early childhood teacher in Massachusetts reflected:

One way I could see my role as a teacher growing with respect to these policies would be asking for consistent and detailed training on online learning platforms. It is now clear that you never know when you will need to use platforms such as SeeSaw to implement lessons and activities, so I would like to be trained before it is needed, rather than in the middle of a crisis. I can definitely envision myself asking administrators to organize this kind of training for teachers and to make sure everyone is prepared to teach in a variety of unconventional ways.

The teacher quoted above had a clear rationale for their own direct policy involvement relating to digital tool training, but was less certain on how exactly to go about this advocacy.

The theme of how to craft and implement digital tool policy more effectively was central to teachers' conversations by the 2021–2022 academic year. Teachers in Massachusetts and in Wisconsin continued to juggle the long-term consequences of digital learning policy developed in the early days of the pandemic and the need for new digital tool policy in response to changing conditions of instruction. Whenever they could, teachers made intentional choices around the type, frequency, and scope of digital tool use, informed by their learnings during remote instruction and their awareness of potential benefits and drawbacks. As evidenced by the narratives shared in this chapter, teachers' digital tool policymaking often happened in the absence of policy directives from district or state entities.

The teachers in our groups in Wisconsin and Massachusetts had informed, well-developed thoughts about existing digital tool policy and its limitations, and about actionable steps for improvement. Teachers' critical questions related to policy design, teachers' nuanced assessments of successes and failures in policy implementation, and their experiences as de facto policy designers through implementation in the classroom clearly position them as policy experts. Yet, this critically important expertise continues to be marginalized in the policy process. Teachers had clear ideas about how to make policy better, but they did not know how and were not invited to put those recommendations into action on a broader scale. The next section details a strategy to help teachers make sense of complex policies, leverage networks and power, and activate policy action plans.

HIGH-LEVERAGE STRATEGY: MAPPING CONCEPTS
AND POWER NETWORKS

Teachers in our groups had clear views on digital tool use. The challenge lay in having access to the kind of policy power that leads to the integration of teacher expertise into policy design. Because they lacked that power, teachers were often left to make policy through practice—a powerful tool, to be sure. However, integrating teachers' expertise into policy design from its inception has the potential to increase policy efficacy. We propose visual mapping as a powerful strategy with two overarching steps: first, crystallizing teachers' values, beliefs, and priorities in a policy area; and second, articulating clear action plans leveraging all available networks and resources. For this strategy in focus, we highlight two different types of maps: concept maps and power network maps, offering examples of how these maps can be used as tools in a range of teacher policy conversations. Though each of the maps can be deployed individually, we recommend using them together, with the concept map laying the groundwork for the subsequent power network map.

Concept Maps

Concept maps are a common pedagogic tool in K–12, higher education, and professional learning spaces. Many educators are familiar with concept maps as a tool for breaking complex ideas into smaller parts and concretizing the relationships between those parts. Here, we advocate their use to help teachers operationalize the concept of "policy and policymaking," and to concretize how they conceive of their own role and relationship to policy, policymaking, and advocacy.

As one of the first activities in our policy advocacy workshops, teachers are given the following prompt: "Draw your conceptualization of how education policy is created and draw where teachers (YOU!) are in this conceptualization." The purpose of this mapping exercise, as seen in Figure 4.1, is to invite teachers to articulate their understandings of the policy process, as well as to articulate their role and responsibility in policymaking.

First, teachers draw their concept maps individually. Once complete, they share them as starting points for small-group discussions with peers, mentor teachers, and teacher educators. This activity can

Figure 4.1. Policy Concept Map

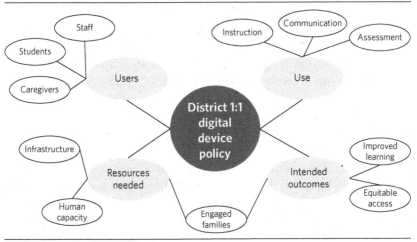

be done both in person and virtually, and with teachers at all levels of experience. If in a face-to-face modality, teachers can put their drawings up on the wall; if virtual, they can do digital drawings and share their screen or use collaborative platforms. In both cases, participants do a "gallery walk" and then come back together for discussion on similarities and differences across visual maps, as well as reflections on what this means about policy and teachers' roles. Participants can then return to their drawings to discuss whether and how their maps have changed.

Teachers learn as much from similarities between their maps and those of peers as they do from differences. This exercise prompts discussion about concepts that are sticky, or ideas that teachers may think are universally understood but in fact have the potential for significant disagreement. The prompt for the visual concept map can vary from context to context. We envision possible concept map prompts including examples such as, "How do you define the idea of policy, and in what policy areas do you see yourself being most interested in advocacy?" We can also see teachers mapping the landscape of issues relating to a specific policy initiative such as "1:1 digital tool policy" or "school discipline and digital device use in school." In all cases, teachers emerge from this exercise with a visual representation of their ideas and a better understanding of how their perspective aligns with or diverges from that of their colleagues.

Power Network Maps

"Power network" maps help make explicit the connections between people and organizations relevant to a policy or social issue (Drew et al., 2011). The purpose of the power network map is to make visible the connections between individuals, groups, and resources that exist in a given policy landscape. This is informative because the machinations of policymaking and hierarchies of power are sometimes obscured; policy can appear as though it simply comes about organically rather than as a result of negotiation and wielding of power. Power network mapping is also useful because it allows participants to see clearly the sources of power they can tap for their own policy priorities. A systematic power network map can elucidate policy levers that may not have been clear before.

In our workshops, participants are asked to select a specific policy area, as seen in Figure 4.2. They are then asked to map all the people and organizations in their network that could bring power to reaching a desired outcome in that area. They place the policy issue in the middle of their map (e.g., lack of transparency around digital platform selection) and then create branches for types of networks (e.g., school district, government, community organizations, families, etc.) stemming from that central policy issue. They then list the names of individual people and organizations from each network branch. As

Figure 4.2. Policy Power Map

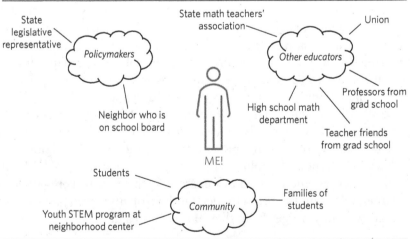

with the concept map, this can be done in person or virtually. Once maps are completed, participants look at one another's maps and discuss similarities and differences along official role, geographic location, district policy context, social identities, and other positionalities. Listing specific people in positions of power and influence is especially important in making explicit who has the authority to make decisions relating to a specific policy issue.

Action Steps

The final phase in visual mapping is to create an action plan. In our workshops, we close the mapping exercise by asking participants to look at their concept map and power network map, and to identify one or two people or organizations to contact in reference to the policy issue of their choosing. The homework for the workshop session involves participants making that contact in the hopes of gaining momentum with that initial step. Visual mapping has specific benefits to building the capacity of teachers as policy advocates. Mapping provides a space for teachers to concretize their substantial policy expertise in a tangible way. Because their policy knowledge is so often overlooked or viewed as less legitimate than other forms of knowledge, visual representations of teachers' deep, multifaceted understanding of policy concepts can serve as tangible reminders of their expertise.

The mapping of relationships across policy concepts also prompts clarifying discussions about why things are the way they are and what would be needed for change. For example, when drawing a concept map of policy and policymaking, teachers often put themselves on the bottom of a hierarchical process. Seeing this visually forces teachers to think about why they place themselves in that conceptual space and invites conversation about informal, formal, individual, and collective policy power. Teachers from different subject areas, grade levels, schools, and districts can talk about why their maps look the way they do.

As described above, the identification of networks prompts teachers to locate potential allies and sources of power and resources in ways that might not immediately have been evident (see Chapter 3). In discussing their power network maps together in a preservice teacher workshop, a preservice teacher in Wisconsin said they newly realized the power in the people they know. Ideally, the maps also remind teachers that they themselves wield power, both individually and collectively; a group of teachers coming together is also a powerful network. When teachers look at others' maps and discuss similarities, differences, and opportunities for coalition building, they not only see that they are not alone in their investment in policy, but see the potential that exists in groups of teachers coming together around shared policy interests. In this way, mapping as a strategy can ignite and support the coalition-building strategy we describe in a previous chapter.

Finally, mapping provides a path for teachers to create an action plan and communicate that action plan to others. It breaks the work of policy advocacy, which often feels overwhelming and distant, down into smaller, more immediate individual steps. When working in groups around a specific policy problem, teachers can team up to tackle next steps together, or to strategically assign action steps so as to minimize the burden on any one individual and maximize the impact of their efforts.

The data we share in this chapter indicate that what teachers wanted was a pathway to integrate their views into policy texts, design, implementation, and evaluation. Teachers' expertise around digital tool use led to a natural question: Once teachers have a recommendation for policy improvement, how do they advocate for its adoption? Using the concept map offers teachers clarity around their views and beliefs. Using the power network map allows them to identify the key decision-makers who can help make change happen. Action steps selected intentionally and collaboratively to contact decision-makers, to share teacher recommendations, and to ask for collaborative action supports meaningful change. Though advocacy is always daunting, this final step of the mapping exercise is a manageable first step that has the potential for impact and for snowballing additional advocacy.

We have applied the strategy of visual mapping to a variety of policy issues. In doing this activity with preservice special education teachers in Wisconsin, for example, teachers focused on policy problems most relevant to them, such as funding for special education assistants in classrooms, the format of the IEP process, the continuum of services provided to students with disabilities, and options for dealing with student behaviors. Participants discussed patterns in the people (other teachers or staff, parents/families, students, administrators, case managers, lawmakers), organizations, or groups (PTAs, school boards, unions, community or activist groups) identified in their networks. Teachers also discussed similarities in the underlying root causes of specific policy issues, such as persistent underfunding of public services, as a core cause for many of the staffing issues listed in the maps. Identifying commonalities across maps increased motivation for collective action related to issues of interest, and in some cases directly led to teachers in common settings (e.g., same district or professional organization) identifying a specific person they were going to contact about an issue. In one session, a group of teachers from the same school created an action plan for changing a building-level policy related to when students could be in the hallway. Mapping the loci of policy power in local communities made clear that it is not only policymakers in Congress or the governor's office who have power and connections to leverage. Teachers, too, have the power to work individually as well as to call on others for action. Visual mapping has promise in the context of the digital tool use we describe in this chapter as well as in a wide range of other policy issues.

CONCLUSION

The experiences of teachers in Massachusetts and Wisconsin before and during the pandemic reflect four key themes demonstrating why teacher advocacy relating to digital learning policy is critically important. First, teachers can provide invaluable insight into the "problem definition" phase of policymaking. The data presented in this chapter illustrate the extent and depth of teachers' knowledge and insight into the complexities and implications of digital tool use in schools. Their expertise would be instrumental to the crafting of policy texts that accurately identify policy problems and goals and reflect the full policy landscape.

Second, teachers' hands-on knowledge of policy in practice could help avoid some challenges of rollout and pitfalls of implementation. In the case of digital tools, teachers accurately identified a slate of implementation needs, including increasing Internet bandwidth, hotspots for families without Internet access, and flexible seating in classrooms to accommodate personalized learning approaches. Having teachers share these potential problems in advance of implementation saves time, resources, and political capital.

Third, the narratives in this chapter show that teachers are already making digital tool policy. Teachers stepped into the space left by the lack of clear district or school policy, using their professional judgment to create policy in their classrooms. While this freedom ultimately served teachers well in making policy choices tailored to their individual students' needs, it can result in digital tool policy that is unevenly or inequitably applied. The stories shared by teachers in this chapter indicate that policy design that ignores the reality that teachers are already policymakers misses a key opportunity for greater coherence, alignment, and equity.

Lastly, the juxtaposition of teacher reflections on digital learning policies before and during the multiple phases in the COVID-19 pandemic show that teachers have much to offer in applying previous policy lessons to inform current efforts. Learning from earlier phases of virtual learning within the pandemic allowed teachers to identify benefits of digital tool policy. It also gave them insight into the significant limitations to the wholesale use of digital devices and the wide range of programs that proliferated during remote instruction. Our data suggests that incorporating teachers' experiences into the evaluation of ongoing policy initiatives supports policy efficacy.

Visual mapping can provide guidance for teachers to identify how to increase their influence around a specific policy issue. Maps prompt critical thinking about root causes of policy issues, how policies intersect, and how power dynamics play out along all levels. In the case of digital tool use, where teachers had very clear views on effective policy and implementation support, mapping is a valuable tool for helping teachers identify allies and resources of power in shaping future digital policy. Perhaps most importantly, they address teachers' desire for impact by building in action steps.

Digital tool use shows no sign of abating, with new platforms and software packages being developed and marketed to school districts every year. Given that digital tools are here to stay, policymakers would do well to leverage teachers' on-the-ground understanding of past lessons to improve future digital learning policy. As K–12 education continues to move into the digital age, the experiences and expertise of teachers must be at the center of identifying the issues *and* policy solutions.

DISCUSSION QUESTIONS

1. In this chapter, as throughout this book, teachers created policy in their individual classrooms in the absence of official district and school policy texts. When does a "practice"

become a "policy"? What are the implications of the overlap and tension between these two concepts? What is the difference between adapting policies to fit the context and noncompliance?

2. Teachers in this chapter were balancing efficiency, concern about students' screen time, and questions about data use in their decisions about how to implement digital tools once back in their classrooms. How might educational researchers support teachers' decision-making in this area? What opportunities do you see for researchers to make their work accessible and useful to teachers in digital learning policy?

3. Mapping concepts and power networks is a helpful strategy for teachers to make sense of specific policy issues and to identify possible action steps. What are ways that groups of teachers could use mapping to create collective action plans, perhaps in a grade-level team or at a school level?

CHAPTER 5

A Collaborative Model for Teacher Policy Advocacy

Approximately 300,000 teachers and staff left the profession between February 2020 and May 2022 (Bureau of Labor Statistics [BLS], 2022), and the problem of teacher shortages in districts nationwide continues to mount. Typically, 8% of teachers exit the field every year, but in a 2022 poll from the National Education Association, 55% of teachers polled reported considering leaving the profession early (Walker, 2022). The intense stress of the pandemic plays a large role in the ongoing and projected teacher exodus, but there are many other factors predating the pandemic that teachers cite as equally important. Staffing shortages, school shootings, and political battles over what teachers can and cannot teach compound to make teaching today arguably more challenging than ever before.

Policy proposals to address the growing shortage of teachers have garnered heated debate. Some states have temporarily lifted certification requirements to have parents and military veterans step in for teachers. Florida and Arizona have proposed allowing individuals who have not yet earned undergraduate degrees to enter the teaching force. Such proposals betray the lack of respect for teaching that has contributed to perennially low wages and status for educators in districts across the United States. They also bear the mark of decisions made with few, if any, practicing teachers at the design table.

It is not surprising that educational policy texts are written by those who do not teach. As the educational research indicates, the role of teachers in policymaking is largely constrained to making and remaking policy through implementation. At the same time, the narratives in this book show the depth and scale of teachers' policy expertise. The teachers we worked with shared story after story of how they adapted policy on the fly in response to quickly changing contexts, effectively making policy through their daily practice. Their collaborative conversations are rich with evidence of their strategic understanding of policy problems, the roadblocks to implementation, and above all the impact of policy on students. Nevertheless, when we ask teachers in our research groups and workshops to create visuals of the policymaking process, the same teachers who are deeply engaged in policy implementation in their classrooms almost always position themselves below or outside of the structures and organizations they identify as central to policy, such as Congress, state agencies, school boards, and school and district administrators. In our work in Massachusetts and Wisconsin, both preservice and practicing teachers were dubious about their ability to be policy advocates, citing local and systemic barriers to policy involvement.

However, we know that there are policymakers, researchers, and politicians who do recognize the expertise, commitment, and vision required to be a skillful teacher. These decision-makers are aware that investing in the flourishing of good teachers is of primary importance to the success of students and society. They also know that excluding teachers from policy design, advocacy, and evaluation has consequences. Without the input of teachers in the setting of policy agendas and in the writing of policy itself, not to mention the assessment of its efficacy, the results often fail to improve conditions and outcomes for students. When teachers already grappling with the difficult work of education confront ongoing evidence of their lack of agency in the educational policy process that might enable them to make positive changes, leaving the profession can be an appealing option. Students and families suffer.

We believe the kind of teacher advocacy that stretches beyond teachers pushing for their individual students is critically important and in need of substantial support. This concluding chapter proposes a model for teacher policy advocacy built on collaboration among preservice and practicing teachers, school administrators, teacher educators, policymakers, and other stakeholders in educational policy. We affirm the importance of teacher policy engagement at all points of the policy process but focus specifically on policy advocacy for systemic change as a critical area of need. Collectively, we can work toward systems and practices that support teachers to be agentic in their work conditions, to help design effective policies, and to adjust existing policies that are not working.

A NOTE ON SYSTEMIC AND INDIVIDUAL
ACTION FOR CHANGE

In our model, we seek to address explicitly the big picture, systems-level obstacles to teacher policy advocacy: Our message is not one of teachers needing to "do more." We recognize that a fundamental obstacle to supporting teacher policy advocacy in schools, teacher education programs, and research collaborations is the longstanding belief that teachers' policy role should be limited to implementation. Indeed, teacher capacity and agency for policy advocacy may be undesirable to those wielding decision-making power. Therefore, there may be little incentive for large-scale systemic change for the purpose of increasing teacher policy advocacy.

Without a doubt, institutional change is necessary. At the same time, we emphasize the power of the individual—not only the teacher, but the administrator, educational researcher, and teacher educator who care about teacher policy advocacy—to take action toward supporting teacher policy advocacy in schools, districts, and beyond. We argue that local policy change by invested individuals, whether in schools, districts, states, or in higher education settings, can be meaningful and impactful. Those who believe in the importance of teacher policy advocacy, again, a group that must include far more partners than teachers alone, can move the needle in their local contexts while continuing to push for widespread institutional change.

Shifting behaviors within our individual loci of control, however small, has an impact on teacher policy advocacy on two levels. First, intentional adjustments to existing processes and systems can create new spaces and avenues for teacher advocacy. Second, taking teacher policy advocacy into account in local policies and practices signals its value in the educational organization. Changes in policy, incremental though they may be, drive changes in behavior and can increase teacher access to resources, networks, and policy power. Changes in behavior, in turn, drive changes in attitudes and perceptions. Our model provides recommendations for institutional change and action steps for individuals who want to increase teacher policy advocacy even within the existing power and political dynamics. In so doing, our model seeks to increase teacher access to, capacity for, and agency around advocacy for educational policies that are more responsive, just, and equitable for all.

We are driven by the teachers we worked with throughout this project. Teachers want greater self-efficacy, agency, and capacity relating to educational policy advocacy (Derrington & Anderson, 2020). As evidenced throughout this book, they care deeply about policy and its impact on their work as well as on their students' learning and well-being. Teachers want to advocate within and beyond their school buildings on policy issues that matter to them, and they seek opportunities and resources to do so. In the sections that follow, we outline a set of basic conditions necessary for teacher policy advocacy, present our theory of action, identify high-leverage spaces and strategies, and propose reflection questions and next steps for teachers, teacher educators, researchers, and policymakers.

A PROPOSED MODEL FOR COLLABORATIVE PROFESSIONAL LEARNING AND ADVOCACY

From our work with preservice and practicing teachers, we have learned that when meaningful policy advocacy occurs, it tends to take place under the following foundational conditions:

1. Teachers have dedicated time and space with one another to learn about, discuss, and collaborate around policy issues.
2. Teachers have easy access to information and data through multiple sources in order to make informed policy decisions.
3. School structures explicitly support teacher participation in policy design, evaluation, and advocacy.
4. Teachers along the career span, from preservice to veteran, have professional learning opportunities to develop knowledge and competency for policy advocacy.
5. School and societal norms reflect the belief that policy work is part of teachers' professional skill sets.

The conditions described above are important on multiple levels. Symbolically, they legitimize the use of time, space, and resources that are typically used for other forms of teacher professional development. Materially, they offer teachers the opportunity to think deeply about beliefs and experiences with policy and to confer with like-minded peers in home districts or farther afield, and they enable the development of networks of information and power. In doing so,

Figure 5.1. Theory of Action for a Model of Collaborative Learning, Agency, and Advocacy

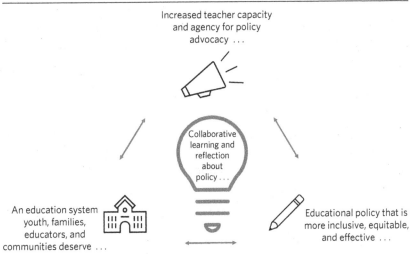

Increased teacher capacity and agency for policy advocacy . . .

Collaborative learning and reflection about policy . . .

An education system youth, families, educators, and communities deserve . . .

Educational policy that is more inclusive, equitable, and effective . . .

these conditions support an increase in teachers' capacity—their self-efficacy, knowledge, skills, and networks—and the likelihood teachers will engage in policy advocacy.

Our theory of action (Figure 5.1) proposes that collaborative learning about policy (the lightbulbs) increases teachers' capacity and agency when it comes to policy advocacy (the megaphone), leading to better educational policy (the pencil), which ultimately contributes to the education system students deserve and communities need (the schoolhouse). This theory of action is based on the belief that policy in which teachers have had a hand is more likely to be aligned with the needs of those who are most directly impacted by educational decision-making. Effective and just policy has a reach beyond individuals. We contend that an increase in teacher engagement in policy advocacy can contribute not only to educational policy that is more responsive to the needs of a wider range of students, families, educators, and communities, but also to a stronger and more equitable educational system.

LOCI OF INFLUENCE AND STRATEGIES FOR ACTION

Any change requires movement at both the institutional and individual levels. Organizations and the decision-makers that comprise them must be held accountable for change, but the actions of policy stakeholders who are "downstream" cannot be contingent on power-sharing from above. Therefore, our model centers on two areas of action, both important and dependent on the other: first, high-leverage spaces, and second, high-leverage strategies for encouraging, supporting, and sustaining teacher policy advocacy.

High-Leverage Spaces to Support the Model

We identify four high-leverage spaces in which to focus our efforts when supporting teacher policy advocacy and include initial questions for consideration and reflection.

Teacher Education. If teacher educators tackle teacher policy advocacy as a topic in teacher preparation, policy advocacy will take its place as a component of teacher professional practice from the earliest stages of the career span. Just as they master content area knowledge, preservice teachers can develop policy knowledge that will support them at all stages of the policy cycle. They can practice policy advocacy in the same way that they practice other teaching strategies. As the data from Chapter 1 indicates, if teacher educators engage their students in conversation around educational policy issues and provide opportunities to practice policy advocacy, preservice teachers will have a greater likelihood of entering the field more aware, more self-efficacious, and with more capacity to advocate for and against policy in their schools and districts. If teacher education programs choose to offer coursework and apprenticeship around policy, just as they offer it around other aspects of teachers' work, preservice teachers are more likely to view teacher policy advocacy as normative.

Teacher educators invested in supporting policy advocacy might first consider the following questions when reflecting on how to move forward:

1. What do you need to know about policy advocacy?
2. What opportunities do you have to increase teacher candidates' exposure to policy advocacy as an element of teacher preparation? What about opportunities to collaborate with one another?
3. Who at your institution can you advocate to in order for policy to be a regular part of the teacher preparation process,

including expectations around competencies gained by being in your program?

4. What educational policy issues matter most to you?
5. Who can be a mentor to preservice teachers in policy advocacy? Are there practicing teachers, professors, or others you know who can serve as a policy advocacy mentor to preservice teachers?
6. Are there student organizations at your program or university that focus on policy?
7. Which of the focus strategies in this book might be most useful to you in your teacher policy advocacy goals?
8. How can you advance your program's broader organizational goals by advancing teacher policy advocacy skills?

District and State Administrative Decision-Making. As the data in Chapter 3 demonstrate, teachers want relationships of trust with administrators who demonstrate respect for their policy expertise by creating meaningful opportunities for discussion and input. If state and district administrators prioritize professional development for policy advocacy, there will be more time, space, and legitimacy afforded to teacher policy engagement. Teachers in Wisconsin and Massachusetts recommended the use of professional development time already built into the school year for policy topics. While time will always be at a premium in schools, dedicating existing professional development time for teachers to learn how to be policy designers, advocates, and evaluators will not only support teachers' skill development, but will signal administrators' awareness of the importance of advocacy as a part of teacher practice.

Those involved in this space of district and state decision-making and invested in supporting policy advocacy might first consider the following questions when reflecting on how to move forward:

1. What avenues exist in your organization for teachers to advocate for policy on a systemic level? Are those avenues equitably accessible to all teachers?
2. Where can you create spaces for teacher voice in the decision-making spaces you have control over? What levers can you pull to engage teachers' policy perspectives?
3. What do you know about what educational policy issues matter most to teachers in your state/district, and how do you know?

4. What organizations and networks do you/can you use to better connect with teachers?
5. Which of the focus strategies in this book might be most useful to you in your teacher policy advocacy goals?
6. How might teacher policy advocacy support your broader organizational goals?

School Decision-Making. At the school level, if principals build systems that assume teacher involvement in school policy conversations as the default, teachers will have greater and more inclusive access to decision-making. For example, as the narratives in Chapter 2 indicate, teachers in Wisconsin and Massachusetts were active in team-level discussions because of the time, space, and official approval granted to team meetings, and they chose to use some of that time to commiserate together about policy. Our teacher collaborators identified effective examples of dedicated time during schoolwide meetings to discuss policy, but these were rare and isolated. Though classroom teachers' policy input rarely extended beyond the grade-level teams, they noted that teacher leaders' official roles offered them a clear pathway to building-level decision-making. For other teachers to have access to building-level policy conversations, they needed to circuit concerns through the teacher leader for dissemination to administrators. Creating structured, inclusive pathways for all teachers, not simply those with designated leadership roles, to share their feedback on policy will result in increased access and can support schools' continuous improvement goals.

Those, like principals, who are involved in this space of school-level decision-making invested in supporting policy advocacy might first consider the following questions when reflecting on how to move forward:

1. What do you know about what educational policy issues matter most to teachers in your school, and how do you know?
2. What avenues exist in your school for teachers to advocate for policy beyond their individual classroom? Are those avenues equitably accessible to all teachers?
3. Where can you create spaces for teacher voice in the decision-making spaces you have control over?

4. How can you advocate for teacher voice in district decision making? What about state or federal?
5. Which of the strategies might be most useful to you in your teacher policy advocacy goals?
6. Who at your school are potential collaborators?
7. What organizations and networks would be helpful to teachers engaging in policy advocacy?
8. Which of the focus strategies in this book might be most useful to you in your teacher policy advocacy goals?

Educational Research. Research partnerships in which researchers avail themselves of the experiences of teachers are plentiful. But the kind of collaboration between researchers and practicing and preservice teachers we envision includes a reciprocal sharing of knowledge that benefits all parties. Researchers and teachers should have equal access and control over the information, networks, and other resources emerging from the work. These dynamics improve access to knowledge, the research process, and the policy the work hopes to inform. The ripple effects of such changes have the potential to be substantial. As Tseng argues, "Democratizing evidence would foster an informed citizenry, in which those furthest from opportunity could influence the development and use of evidence to drive stronger government, policy, and practice" (Tseng, 2020).

Educational researchers who argue for the importance of teacher policy advocacy must also amplify evidence of the impact of teacher policy advocacy. Any findings useful to teachers must be clear and easily accessible. In addition to democratizing how we do the work as educational researchers, we also must democratize the way we communicate and disseminate it. For example, teams of researchers and teachers can coauthor op-eds about specific policy issues. (e.g., mental health supports in schools) or the policymaking process itself (e.g., role of teacher voice in district policymaking).

Participatory action research (PAR), as another example, offers a structure that centers those closest to the work itself in designing and conducting research studies, as well as acting on what is learned (Chevalier & Buckles, 2013; Feldman et al., 2018; Mertler, 2009). In this case, teachers can partner with researchers in setting research agendas and framing of research questions related to how policy interacts with their work, identities, and the conditions surrounding schools. The cointerpretation of data is another high-leverage space for collaboration, where teachers can drive the process of sensemaking from patterns in the data. PAR can facilitate collective reflection toward collective action with the ultimate goal of liberatory practices, policies, and systemic change (Freire, 1970). This embodies a critical policy approach in which "conducting critical policy work becomes a type of active advocacy, rather than passive scholarship, wherein education scholars are working alongside their communities to actually do critical policy work and engage democratic processes on the ground" (Welton & Mansfield, 2020, p. 3).

Those involved in this space of educational research and invested in supporting policy advocacy might first consider the following questions when reflecting on how to move forward:

1. If you study schools, teaching, and/or educational policymaking, what role do practicing or preservice teachers have in influencing:
   a. your study design?
   b. the interpretation of data?
   c. the communication of findings and recommendations?
2. How will your work change systems and structures?
3. Which of the focus strategies in this book might be most useful to you in your teacher policy advocacy goals?
4. How are you communicating your findings in a way that is accessible and useful to educators/school leaders?

Each of the educational spaces detailed above represents a locus of policy action. Individuals within these spaces can impact decisions around professional development seminars on policy advocacy, opportunities for teachers to provide feedback on policy in open fora, the creation of educational policy courses in teacher education, and elsewhere. When teachers learn about educational policy in their training programs, when sharing feedback about policy is expected in schools, when policy training is part of district professional development, when external groups engage with teachers around policy materials and resources, and when educational policy research includes teachers, teacher policy advocacy has the chance to be a more substantive, integrated, and legitimated part of teacher professional practice. Together, these efforts comprise the ecosystem in which teachers' efforts in policymaking can thrive or languish. Synergy across these spaces can result in a powerful positive impact on the development of teacher policy advocacy by contributing to an educational system in which teacher input in educational policy is the standard rather than the exception.

High-Leverage Strategies to Support the Model

Throughout this book, we employ teachers' experiences as the landscape against which to set four focal strategies for increasing teacher policy advocacy. Our data suggest that the strategies show promise in supporting teachers' increased capacity and agency for advocacy. For example, one preservice teacher reflected on the impact of collaborative mentorship on their own thinking and practice:

> My interactions with policy have also grown simply in the fact that I am having conversations about policy with my [supervising practitioner]. This allows me to think critically about the ways in which policy affects educators and students, and I don't think I would be thinking as much about it if I were not having these conversations with my supervising teacher.

The strategies we highlight in this book are especially valuable because they are applicable to a broad range of policy environments and school contexts. Although the strategies vary in scope and level of involvement, they share the following set of key characteristics.

1. They are built on the premise that teacher policy advocacy is beneficial to successful, effective educational policy.
2. They are all open to collaboration, inviting participation from multiple groups of policy participants.
3. They provide a structure with room for coconstructed frameworks and responsiveness to participant needs.
4. They are flexible and allow for asynchronous and online participation.
5. They range in resource use along time, space, coordination, and financial support.

Though each of the strategies can be implemented as a stand-alone approach to supporting teacher policy advocacy in a particular setting, we offer them as a slate of strategies that can also be implemented together. In the list that follows, we present the strategies in order of ascending demands on resources and structure.

> *Mapping.* Teachers draw "maps," or visual representations of how concepts, networks, people, organizations, and power connect to policy issues.
>
> *Coalition Building.* Teachers build connections, resources, and power with fellow teachers, families, students, unions, researchers, and community groups.
>
> *Collaborative Mentorship.* Teachers engage in a structured and collaborative mentoring approach in identifying, analyzing, and potentially participating in advocacy around specific educational policies relevant in their day-to-day work.
>
> *EdCamps.* Teachers convene day-long "unconferences" that center teachers as experts and prioritize connections and dialogue.

Successful collaboration does not have to include each of the strategies described in this book. For example, teachers can use concept and network power mapping to visualize their beliefs, attitudes, and experiences relating to policy. The maps can serve as starting points for individual reflection and deep discussion with teachers across grade levels, districts, and career points. Teachers can create individual and collective action plans, where they identify potential collaborators (e.g., other educators, families, students) with whom they can build coalitions. These coalitions, in turn, can result in the convening of EdCamps and support wider networks of information and resources sharing both in person and in virtual settings. Conversely, teachers can organize an EdCamp where mapping and action plans are part of collective discussion, or they can establish a collaborative mentoring initiative through informal networks with their professional organization or their grade-level team. Given the demands of teaching in the current sociopolitical context, flexibility, ease of access, and efficacy are of paramount importance in this model.

At the same time, multiple strategies can be combined for additional impact. Mapping, particularly power network mapping, can lead to more intentional coalition building across groups. Collaborative mentoring partnerships can emerge out of sessions at EdCamps. All four strategies can be layered upon one another in a school or district to create multiple modalities for teacher professional development relating to policy advocacy.

Figure 5.2. High-Leverage Spaces and Strategies for Collaborative Learning, Agency, and Advocacy

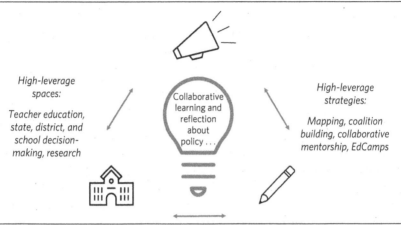

An EdCamp in the winter of 2021–2022 offers an example of how coalition building and EdCamp strategies go hand-in-hand. At this event, over 100 teachers met either in person or virtually. Teachers at the in-person session spent the first hour in informal ice breaker–type activities, meeting one another and making connections. The rest of the day was spent in small-group sessions on topics such as family engagement, gamification, teacher wellness, education policy, and authentic assessment. Throughout the day, teachers in both the in-person and virtual environments communicated, connected, and shared resources via active discussions and posts on Twitter and in shared Google docs. EdCamps like this offer not only an opportunity for sharing of ideas, but also building of individual relationships and collective networks that can facilitate broader advocacy.

Note, too, that the responsibility for initiating any of these strategies does not lie solely with teachers. Teachers can certainly opt to implement any of the four strategies of their own accord or with like-minded peers in their schools. However, as we shared in the section on high-leverage spaces, teacher educators, researchers, administrators, and policy stakeholders in other settings can and should take the lead in setting a strategy in motion. The symbolic and material responsibility for action must be shared, as illustrated in Figure 5.2.

Impact on Practice

In addition to the examples shared in this book, our model has been adapted for a variety of other teacher groups and contexts, ranging from a break-out session in a university-based summer institute for early career teachers to a daylong summer professional learning workshop with a statewide educational content organization. Sustained, deep learning for student and practicing teachers requires a comprehensive approach with many points of entry and across many contexts. Across these settings, teachers we have worked with report that the model is impactful. The maps crystallize their conceptions of where policy power resides and where their own work sits in relation to that power. The conversations that bubble to the surface when policy is explicitly prioritized as a professional development topic reflect their nuanced and informed perspectives on any number of educational policies. Teachers identify policy needs, obstacles to their full participation as advocates, and resources that would support their greater involvement. In conversation with one another, they see evidence of themselves as policy experts and policymakers. Ultimately, they feel greater self-efficacy as policy advocates and express interest in navigating advocacy in community and collaboration with like-minded peers. In response to the prompt, "What is one action step you can/will take after participating in these sessions?" preservice teachers gave concrete examples drawing on strategies including collaborative mentorship, coalition building, and mapping their networks:

> Talking to my cooperating teacher about the advocacy work she is involved in.

> I will subscribe to more local news sources, follow advocates for educational policy on social media, and ask my CT more questions about the current policies and proposed policies affecting [the district].

> Look on social media to see if there are any of my teacher friends that are involved with community policy changes and look into what I can do to help.

> One action step I can take is making sure I make connections when I start my new position so that I can go to them when needed.

In reflecting on the impact on her own sense of agency, a practicing teacher in Massachusetts explained, "I think I've become more aware that I can do something about a policy that I don't like. Now it's like, I actually could probably do something about it, or at least try to. So, I feel like this little thing has put that in the back of my mind." Another practicing teacher agreed, stating:

> By participating in this, it has made me as a teacher more aware of policies and how they affect teachers on a daily basis. It has also encouraged me to talk with my colleagues and student teacher about different policies, our roles in these policies and how we can evoke change. . . . I've had more discussions during lunch and during my prep time on policies that affect the Kindergarten team, school, and community.

COLLECTIVE ACTION FOR CHANGE

There is promise in the teacher feedback presented above. Still, none of the strategies we discuss can be a panacea, because problems of educational practice are complex. It is tempting to wish for perfect outcomes in which teachers and other educational partners magically come together to effect broad change that results in teacher experts in every policy discussion. Indeed, we continue to push for the far-reaching, sweeping systemic changes that would result in a diverse slate of teachers at the center of policy agenda setting, design, advocacy, and evaluation. In the meantime, however, we also focus our attention on fostering the individual efforts of people in the high-leverage spaces we describe above. We believe that through the application of one or more strategies, and in collaboration with others, individuals can shift policies within their spheres of influence toward supporting teacher policy advocacy while continuing to push for broad, institutionalized support.

Teacher advocacy around educational policy has far-reaching implications. Policy affects the structures, processes, and outcomes of societal institutions, including but not limited to education, as well as the prospects of democracy in general. Strengthening policy advocacy across preservice teacher education and the K–12 field has the potential for a number of positive changes in how policy is made, applied, and evaluated. Greater teacher policy advocacy can lead to

positive shifts in how teachers and schools are framed in policy discourse, a better match between policies and the contexts in which
they are implemented, greater consistency between policy text and
policy in practice, and more realistic expectations for policy reforms.
When asked what teachers need to feel more fully supported in the
classroom, the 2022 National Teacher of the Year, Kurt Russell, re-
plied, "You know what? That's a great question. I think we need just
to feel respected. A lot of times we have policies that go against the
fundamentals of teaching . . . I think teachers are the experts in the
classroom. And we need to be treated as such" (Bennett et al., 2022).

Ultimately, we believe teacher policy advocacy can motivate
meaningful changes that directly affect students, schools, teachers,
and the profession of teacher education. It is our hope this book will
increase teacher policy advocacy, not only because policy is better
when teachers are involved in its design, but because the personal and
professional flourishing of teachers is central to the success of our
schools and society.

References

Addington, L. A. (2009). Cops and cameras: Public school security as a policy response to Columbine. *American Behavioral Scientist, 52*(10), 1426–1446. https://doi.org/10.1177/0002764209332556

Aghasaleh, R. (2018). Oppressive curriculum: Sexist, racist, classist, and homophobic practice of dress codes in schooling. *Journal of African American Studies, 22*, 94–108. https://doi.org/10.1007/s12111-018-9397-5

Ambrosetti, A., & Dekkers, J. (2010). The interconnectedness of the roles of mentors and mentees in pre-service teacher education mentoring relationships. *Australian Journal of Teacher Education, 35*(6). http://dx.doi.org/10.14221/ajte.2010v35n6.3

American Civil Liberties Union. (n.d.). *School-to-prison pipeline.* Accessed July 23, 2021 from https://www.aclu.org/issues/juvenile-justice/school-prison-pipeline

Anderson, G. (1989). Critical ethnography in education: Origins, current status, and new directions. *Review of Educational Research, 59*(3), 249–270.

Au, W. (2009). *Unequal by design: High-stakes testing and the standardization of inequality.* Routledge.

Ball, S. (2006). What is policy? Texts, trajectories and toolboxes. In S. Ball (Ed.), *Education policy and social class: The selected works of Stephen Ball* (pp. 43–53). Routledge. (Original work published 1993)

Ball, S. (2006). *Education policy and social class: The selected works of Stephen Ball.* Routledge.

Barber, M., & Mourshed, M. (2007). *How the world's best-performing school systems come out on top.* McKinsey & Co.

Behizadeh, N., Thomas, C., & Cross, S. (2017). Reframing for social justice: The influence of critical friendship groups on preservice teachers' reflective practice. *Journal of Teacher Education, 70*(3). https://doi.org/10.1177/0022487117737306

Bennett, G., Mufson, C., & Corkery, A. (2022, May 1). *2022 National Teacher of the Year Kurt Russell discusses the joys and challenges his job.* PBS.org. https://www.pbs.org/newshour/show/2022-national-teacher-of-the-year-kurt-russell-discusses-the-joys-and-challenges-his-job

Bensimon, E., & Marshall, C. (2003). Like it or not: Feminist critical policy analysis matters. *Journal of Higher Education, 74*(3), 337–349. https://doi.org/10.1080/00221546.2003.11780850

Borum, R., Cornell, D., Modzeleski, W., & Jimerson, S. (2009). What can be done about school shootings? A review of the evidence. *Educational Researcher, 39*(1), 27. https://doi.org/10.3102/0013189X09357620

Bowe, R., Ball, S., & Gold, A. (1992). *Reforming education and changing schools: Case studies in policy sociology.* Routledge.

Bureau of Labor and Statistics. (2022). *Occupational outlook handbook: Education, training, and library occupations.* Retrieved June 1, 2022, from https://www.bls.gov/ooh/education-training-and-library/home.htm

Catapano, S. (2006). Teaching in urban schools: Mentoring pre-service teachers to apply advocacy strategies. *Mentoring & Tutoring, 14*(1), 81–96. https://doi.org/10.1080/13611260500432756

Chase, M., Dowd, A., Pazich, L., & Bensimon, E. (2014). Transfer equity for "minoritized" students: A critical policy analysis of seven states. *Educational Policy, 28*(5), 669–717. https://doi.org/10.1177/0895904812468227

Chevalier, J. M. & Buckles, D. J. (2013). *Participatory action research: Theory and methods for engaged inquiry.* Routledge UK.

Chingos, M. (2012, November 29). *Strength in numbers: State spending on K-12 assessment systems.* Brookings Institution. https://www.brookings.edu/research/strength-in-numbers-state-spending-on-k-12-assessment-systems/

Coburn, C. E. (2001). Collective sensemaking about reading: How teachers mediate reading policy in their professional communities. *Educational Evaluation and Policy Analysis, 23*(2), 145–170.

Conley, S. (1991). Review of research on teacher participation in school decision making. *Review of Research in Education, 17,* 225–266.

Coffman, A. (2015). Teacher agency and education policy. *The New Educator, 11*(4), 322–332. https://doi.org/10.1080/1547688X.2015.1087759

Delgado, A., Wardlow, L., McKnight, K., & O'Malley, K. (2015). Educational technology: A review of the integration, resources, and effectiveness of technology in K-12 classrooms. *Journal of Information Technology Education: Research, 14,* 397–416.

Derrington, M. L., & Anderson, L. (2020). Expanding the role of teacher leaders: Professional learning for policy advocacy. *Education Policy Analysis Archives, 28*(68). https://doi.org/10.14507/epaa.28.4850

DeSimone, D. (2022). *COVID-19 infections by race: What's behind the health disparities?* Mayo Clinic. https://www.mayoclinic.org/diseases-conditions/coronavirus/expert-answers/coronavirus-infection-by-race/faq-20488802

Diem, S., Young, M., Welton, A., Mansfield, K., & P. L. Lee. (2014). The intellectual landscape of critical policy analysis. *International Journal of Qualitative Studies in Education, 27*(9), 1068–1090. https://doi.org/10.1080/09518398.2014.916007

Drew, R., Aggleton, P., Chalmers, H., & Wood, K. (2011). Using social network analysis to evaluate a complex policy network. *Evaluation, 17*(4), 383–394. https://doi.org/10.1177/1356389011421699

Dubetz, N. E., & de Jong, E. J. (2011). Teacher advocacy in bilingual programs. *Bilingual Research Journal, 34*(3), 248–262. https://doi.org/10.1080/15235882.2011.623603

Edmondson, J. (2004). Reading policies: Ideologies and strategies for political engagement. *Reading Teacher, 57*(5), 418–428.

Ellis, N., Alonzo, D., & Nguyen, H. T. M. (2020). Elements of a quality pre-service teacher mentor: A literature review. *Teaching and Teacher Education, 92*. https://doi.org/10.1016/j.tate.2020.103072

Eppley, K. (2009). Rural schools and the highly qualified teacher provision of No Child Left Behind: A critical policy analysis. *International Journal of Qualitative Studies in Education, 27*(9), 1068–1090.

Everytown for Gun Safety. (n.d.). *Which states don't allow teachers or the general public to carry guns in K–12 schools?* Retrieved June 1, 2022, from https://everytownresearch.org/rankings/law/no-guns-in-k-12-schools/

Fairbanks, C. M., Freedman, D., & Kahn, C. (2000). The role of effective mentors in learning to teach. *Journal of Teacher Education, 51*(2), 102–112.

Feldman, A., Altrichter, H., Posch, P., & Somekh, B. (2018). *Teachers investigate their work: An introduction to action research across the professions.* Routledge.

Feiman-Nemser, S. (2003). What new teachers need to learn. *Educational Leadership, 60*(8), 25–29.

Fernández, M. B. (2018). Framing teacher education: Conceptions of teaching, teacher education, and justice in Chilean national policies. *Education Policy Analysis Archives, 26*(34), 34.

Freire, P. (1970). *Pedagogy of the oppressed.* Continuum.

Fry, R. (2022, January 14). *Some gender disparities widened in the U.S. workforce during the pandemic.* Pew Research Center. https://www.pewresearch.org/fact-tank/2022/01/14/some-gender-disparities-widened-in-the-u-s-workforce-during-the-pandemic/

Gale, T., & Densmore, K. (2003). Democratic educational leadership in contemporary times. *International Journal of Leadership in Education, 6*(2), 119–136. https://doi.org/10.1080/13603120304819

Gillborn, D. (2005). Education policy as an act of white supremacy: Whiteness, critical race theory, and education reform. *Journal of Education Policy 20*(4), 485–505. https://doi.org/10.1080/02680930500132346

Good, A. (2019). *Teachers at the table: Voice, agency, and advocacy in educational policymaking.* Lexington Books, Rowman, and Littlefield.

Good, A., Barocas, S. F., Chavez-Moreno, L., Feldman, R., & Canela, C. (2017). A seat at the table: How the work of teaching impacts teachers as policy agents. *Peabody Journal of Education, 92*(4), 505–520.

Good, A., Hara, M., Dryer, G., & Harper, J. (2020). Teachers and educational policy advocacy: Capacity, agency, and implications for practice. In E. Ethridge, J. Davis & C. Winterbottom (Eds.), *Advocacy in education: Research-based strategies for teachers, administrators, parents, and the community.* Nova Science Publishers.

Greenawalt, J., Ivery, J., Mizrahi, T., & Rosenthal, B. (2021). Coalitions and Coalition Building. In *Encyclopedia of social work.* https://oxfordre.com/socialwork/view/10.1093/acrefore/9780199975839.001.0001/acrefore-9780199975839-e-1423

Hall, K., Draper, R., Smith, L., & Bullough, R. (2008). More than a place to teach: Exploring the perceptions of the roles and responsibilities of mentor teachers. *Mentoring & Tutoring: Partnership in Learning, 16*(3), 328–345. https://doi.org/10.1080/13611260802231708

Hara, M. (2020). Safety, advocacy, and the teacher's role: Pre-service teachers and school shooting policies. *Education Policy Analysis Archives, 28*(31). https://doi.org/10.14507/epaa.28.4800

Heineke, A. J., Ryan, A. M., & Tocci, C. (2015). Teaching, learning, and leading: Preparing teachers as educational policy actors. *Journal of Teacher Education, 66*(4), 382–394.

Heinrich, C., Darling-Aduana, J., & Good, A. (2020). *Equity and quality in digital learning: Realizing the promise in K–12 education.* Harvard Education Press.

Henry, M. (1993). What is policy? A response to Stephen Ball. *Discourse, 14*(1), 102–105.

Hertz, M. B. (2010, September 29). Introduction to Edcamp: A new conference model built on collaboration. *Edutopia.* http://www.edutopia.org/blog/about-edcamp-unconference-history

Hurwitz, S., Garman-McClaine, B., & Carlock, K. (2021). Special education for students with autism during the COVID-19 pandemic: "Each day brings new challenges." *Autism, 26*(4), 889–899. https://doi.org/10.1177/13623613211035935

Ingersoll, R. (2006). *Who controls teachers' work? Power and accountability in America's schools.* Harvard University Press.

Ishimaru, A. M. (2022). Possible futures: Youth, families, and communities as educational leaders. *Phi Delta Kappan, 103*(1), 38–42. https://kappanonline.org/possible-futures-youth-families-communities-leaders-ishimaru/

Jekielek, S., Brown, B., Marin, P., & Lippman, L. (2007, September). *Public school practices for violence prevention and reduction: 2003–04* (Issue Brief No. NCES2007-010). National Center for Education Statistics. https://nces.ed.gov/pubs2007/2007010.pdf

Johnson, A. (2017, October 25). Bill aims to protect teachers from assault; critics say it will boost school-to-prison pipeline. *Milwaukee Journal Sentinel.* https://www.jsonline.com/story/news/education/2017/10/25/bill-aims-protect-teachers-assault-critics-say-boost-school-to-prison-pipeline/794635001/

Jones, D., Khalil, D., & Dixon, D. (2017). Teacher-advocates respond to ESSA: "Support the good parts—resist the bad parts." *Peabody Journal of Education, 92*(4), 445–465. https://doi.org/10.1080/0161956X.2017.1349479

Khalid, A. (2013, December 3). *Massachusetts students among top-performing in global exam.* WBUR. https://www.wbur.org/news/2013/12/03/massachusetts-pisa-test-results

Knipp, H., & Stevenson, R. (2021). "A powerful visual statement": Race, class, and gender in uniform and dress code policies in New Orleans public charter schools. *Affilia, 37*(1), 79–96. https://doi.org/10.1177/08861099211010026

Kram, K. (1985). *Mentoring at work.* Scott, Foresman.

Kremer, R. (2019, October 30). *Wisconsin has widest achievement gap on nation's report card.* Wisconsin Public Radio. https://www.wpr.org/wisconsin-has-widest-achievement-gap-nations-report-card

Lawson, H., Jones, E., Beddoes, Z., Estes, S., Morris, S., Mitchell, M., van der Mars, H., & Ward, P. (2021). Collective action for learning, improvement, and redesign. *Journal of Teaching in Physical Education*, 40(3), 412–422. https://doi.org/10.1123/jtpe.2020-0246

Lisowski, O. (2018, January 12). *Wisconsin moves to end violence against teachers in the classroom*. MacIver Institute. https://www.maciverinstitute.com/2018/01/wisconsin-moves-to-end-violence-against-teachers-in-the-classroom/

Lopez, A. (2013). Collaborative mentorship: A mentoring approach to support and sustain teachers for equity and diversity. *Mentoring and Tutoring: Partnership in Learning*, 21(3), 292–311. https://doi.org/10.1080/13611267.2013.827836

Lynch, M. (2016, July 5). What you need to know about standardized assessments [Opinion]. *Education Week*. https://www.edweek.org/education/opinion-what-you-need-to-know-about-standardized-assessments/2016/07

Maguire, M., Braun, A., & Ball, S. J. (2015). "Where you stand depends on where you sit": The social construction of policy enactments in the (English) secondary school." *Discourse, 36*(4): 485–499. https://doi.org/10.1080/01596306.2014.977022

Mapp, K., & Bergman, E. (2021). *Embracing a new normal: Toward a more liberatory approach to family engagement*. Carnegie Corporation of New York. https://media.carnegie.org/filer_public/f6/04/f604e672-1d4b-4dc3-903d-3b619a00cd01/fe_report_fin.pdf

Marshall, C. (1997). *Feminist critical policy analysis: A perspective from primary and secondary schooling*. Routledge.

Massachusetts Department of Education. (n.d.). *Data and accountability*. Retrieved June 2, 2022 from www.doe.mass.edu/DataAccountability.html

Massachusetts Gen. Laws Ch 140, § 121–131Q (2014). Massachusetts Firearms Laws. https://malegislature.gov/Laws/GeneralLaws/PartI/TitleXX/Chapter140/Section121

McKinney de Royston, M., & Turner, E. O. (2020, September 2). *Acting collectively and systematically for equity in pandemic schooling* [Opinion]. Cap Times. https://madison.com/opinion/article_3ad46959-69b3-5e61-bf2f-b4a9795c3528.html

McLaren, P., & Giarelli, J. (1995). *Critical theory and educational research*. State University of New York Press.

Mertler, C. (2009). *Action research: Teachers as researchers in the classroom*. Sage.

Nettles, M., Scatton, L., Steinberg, J., & Tyler, L. (2011). *Performance and passing rate differences of African American and White prospective teachers on Praxis™ Examinations*. Educational Testing Service and National Education Association. https://doi.org/10.1002/j.2333-8504.2011.tb02244.x

Niesz, T., & D'Amato, R. (2021). Social media connections between educators and advocacy networks: The Twitter activity of teacher activist groups. In M. Griffin & C. Zinskie (Eds.), *Social media: Influences on education* (pp. 299–336). Information Age Publishers.

Noddings, N. (1996). The caring professional. In S. Gordon, P. Benner & N. Noddings (Eds.), *Caregiving: Readings in knowledge, practice, ethics, and politics*. University of Pennsylvania Press.

Noguera, P. A. (1995). Preventing and Producing Violence: A Critical Analysis of Responses to School Violence. *Harvard Educational Review, 65*(2), 189–212.

Ozga, J. (1987). *Schoolwork: Approaches to the labor of teaching.* McGraw-Hill.

Petchauer, E. (2012). Teacher licensure exams and Black teacher candidates: Toward new theory and promising practice [Special issue]. *The Journal of Negro Education, 81*(3), 252–267. https://doi.org/10.7709/jnegroeducation.81.3.0252

Sayman, D., & Cornell, H. (2021). "Building the plane while trying to fly.": Exploring special education teacher narratives during the COVID-19 pandemic. *Planning and Changing, 50*(3/4), 191–207.

Schreck, C., & Miller, J. (2003). Sources of fear of crime at school: What is the relative contribution of disorder, individual characteristics, and school security? *Journal of School Violence, 2*(4), 57–79. https://doi.org/10.1300/J202v02n04_04

Schroeder, N. L., Nesbit, J. C., Anguiano, C. J., & Adesope, O. O. (2017). Studying and constructing concept maps: A meta-analysis. *Educational Psychology Review, 30*, 431–455.

Scott, E., & J. Grant. (2016). *The school-to-prison pipeline: A legislative database summary.* Howard University. https://walterscenter.howard.edu/sites/walterscenter.howard.edu/files/2021-07/Legislative_Summary_FINAL%20REPORT.pdf

Seelig, M., Millette, D., Zhou, C., & Huang, J. (2019). A New culture of advocacy: And exploratory analysis of social activism on the web and social media. *Atlantic Journal of Communication, 27*(1), 15–29. https://doi.org/10.1080/15456870.2019.1540418

Smith, A. (2007). Mentoring for experienced school principals: Professional learning in a safe space. *Mentoring and Tutoring, 15*(3), 277–291.

Smylie, M. A. (1992). Teacher participation in school decision making: Assessing willingness to participate. *Educational Evaluation and Policy Analysis, 14*(1), 53–67. https://doi.org/10.3102/01623737014001053

Stovall, D. (2013). 14 souls, 19 days and 1600 dreams: Engaging critical race praxis while living on the "edge" of race. *Discourse: Studies in the Cultural Politics of Education, 34*(4), 562–578. https://doi.org/10.1080/01596306.2013.822625

Taylor, D. L., & Bogotch, I. E. (1994). School-level effects of teachers' participation in decision making. *Educational Evaluation and Policy Analysis, 16*(3), 302–319.

Taylor, S. (1997). Critical policy analysis: Exploring contexts, text, and consequences. *Discourse: Studies in the Cultural Politics of Education, 18*(1), 23–35.

Thompson, C. (2021, January 25). *Fatal police shootings of unarmed Black people reveal troubling patterns.* National Public Radio. https://www.npr.org/2021/01/25/956177021/fatal-police-shootings-of-unarmed-black-people-reveal-troubling-patterns

Tseng, V. (2020, November 30). Building trust in science will require democratizing evidence [Opinion]. *The Hill.* https://thehill.com/opinion/education/527921-building-trust-in-science-will-require-democratizing-evidence/

Ujifusa, A. (2012, November 28). Standardized testing costs states $1.7 billion a year, study says. *Education Week*. https://www.edweek.org/teaching-learning /standardized-testing-costs-states-1-7-billion-a-year-study-says/2012/11?tkn =VLMFJUQpeyvKkTzwuCHPd%2FuQG%2BPWLRrD1lNp&cmp=clp -edweek

Ujifusa, A. (2018, March 14). House passes STOP School Violence Act one month after Parkland shooting. *Education Week*. https://www.edweek.org/policy -politics/house-passes-stop-school-violence-act-one-month-after-parkland -shooting/2018/03

Walker, T. (2022, February 1). *Survey: Alarming number of educators may soon leave the profession*. National Education Association. https://www.nea.org /advocating-for-change/new-from-nea/survey-alarming-number-educators -may-soon-leave-profession

Welton, A., & Mansfield, K. (2020). More than just an academic exercise: Conjoining critical policy analysis and community-engaged research as an embodiment of political action. *Educational Studies*, 56(6), 619–635. https://doi .org/10.1080/00131946.2020.1837834

Wisconsin Department of Public Instruction. (2020). *What families need to know about additional services due to extended school closure*. https://dpi.wi.gov /sites/default/files/imce/sped/pdf/covid-additional-services-qa.pdf

Wisconsin Department of Public Instruction. (2020). *Wisconsin Public Schools at a Glance*. https://dpi.wi.gov/sites/default/files/imce/eis/pdf/schools_at_a _glance.pdf

Wisconsin Educator Effectiveness Research Partnership. (2019). *Race, Relational Trust, and Teacher Retention in Wisconsin Schools*. https://uwm.edu/sreed /wp-content/uploads/sites/502/2019/11/WEERP-Brief-Nov-2019-Race -Relational-Trust-and-Teacher-Retention.pdf

Zandvakill, E., Washington, E., & Gordon, E. (2019). Teaching patterns of critical thinking: The 3CA model—Concept maps, critical thinking, collaboration, and assessment. *SAGE Open*, 9(4), 1–15.

Index

The letter *t* after a page number indicates a figure.

About the Authors

May Hara is associate professor of education at Framingham State University and a former middle school English teacher. Her work focuses on the critical role that preservice and practicing teachers play in educational policy.

Annalee G. Good is a scientist at the Wisconsin Center for Education Research at the University of Wisconsin–Madison, where she co-directs the Wisconsin Evaluation Collaborative and the WCER Clinical Program. She is a former middle school social studies teacher.